THE UNOFFICIAL RECIPE GUIDE

The Blackstone Griddle

100 EASY, FLAVORFUL RECIPES to Fuel Your Outdoor Adventures

Cheri Reneé
Author of
The "I Love My Blackstone Griddle" Cookbook

ADAMS MEDIA
NEW YORK AMSTERDAM/ANTWERP LONDON TORONTO
SYDNEY/MELBOURNE NEW DELHI

This book is an independent publication and has not been authorized, approved, licensed, or endorsed by Blackstone Products or its parent company, North Atlantic Imports, LLC. The stylized Blackstone trademark [US Serial Number: 87327816] is registered to North Atlantic Imports, LLC. The publisher makes no claim to any right, title, or interest in this trademark based upon its usage in the book.

Adams Media
An Imprint of Simon & Schuster, LLC
100 Technology Center Drive
Stoughton, MA 02072

First Adams Media hardcover edition October 2025

Interior design by Colleen Cunningham
Photographs by Nathan Rega, Harper Point Photography
Food stylist and chef: Kira Friedman
Chef's assistant: Martine English

Manufactured in the United States of America

1 2025

Library of Congress Control Number: 2025940357

ISBN 978-1-5072-2457-1
ISBN 978-1-5072-2458-8 (ebook)

Always follow safety and commonsense cooking protocols while using kitchen utensils, operating ovens and stoves, and handling uncooked food. If children are assisting in the preparation of any recipe, they should always be supervised by an adult.

CONTENTS

Chapter 5. Camp Main Dishes 81

Chapter 6. Desserts 127

Standard US/Metric Measurement Conversions 149

Index 151

INTRODUCTION

Wish you could spend more time celebrating the outdoors and less time cooking meals?

Want to eat tasty, healthy (and warm) meals instead of cuisine from a box or package?

Looking for your mealtime cleanup to be cut in half?

Then cooking on a Blackstone griddle is the answer you've been searching for! This flat top griddle will completely transform the way you prepare meals during your camping and RV trips.

The large, flat cook space of a griddle allows you to quickly prepare multiple items at once and makes feeding a crowd easy and stress-free. Blackstone griddles come in a wide variety of sizes—some even designed specifically for camping—so they are easily transported to wherever you are headed. Plus, because you use only one appliance instead of switching among multiple ones, the cleanup is super simple, creating more time for all your camping activities!

In *The Blackstone Griddle Camping Cookbook*, you'll discover one hundred tasty, family-friendly recipes for cooking in the great outdoors. You'll find a variety of options from hearty breakfasts and quick camping snacks to complete dinners and effortless lunch ideas. There's also a chapter dedicated to desserts to satisfy your sweet tooth! There are some lighter meals for those hot summer camping days, as well as comfort food options to warm you up on the chillier days. Inside, you'll discover:

- Waffle Breakfast Pizzas
- Lemon Pepper Chicken Wings
- BBQ Onion Ring Burgers

- Spinach and Tomato Ravioli
- Hot Honey Pork and Apples
- Garlic Butter Steak Bites and Potatoes
- Stir-Fried Vegetable Ramen
- Donut Whoopie Pies
- S'mores Banana Splits

These recipes have been created with the understanding that you will be bringing most of your ingredients when you go camping. In fact, most of the recipes have five main ingredients or fewer, so you can pack your cooler or camper refrigerator as minimally as possible. Plus, many of the recipes include optional variations on ways to transform one dish into several versions, so you'll never get bored on your camping adventures. You'll also find appetizing photos and tips on seasoning and cleaning your Blackstone, as well as finding the right accessories to use with your griddle.

Whether you are new to flat top griddle cooking or already a Blackstone master, you will be able to cook warm, delicious, and nutritious meals while still enjoying nature and making camping memories with your friends and family!

CAMP COOKING WITH A BLACKSTONE GRIDDLE

In this chapter, you will learn all about using your flat top griddle. Here you'll find all the important information you need: instructions on seasoning your griddle, descriptions of must-have tools and accessories for camping, helpful tips and tricks for camp cooking, and proper griddle-cleaning techniques. You will soon discover that preparing a whole meal on one surface with controlled heat and easy cleanup makes any camping trip much more enjoyable!

Blackstone Griddle Basics

A Blackstone griddle is a flat steel cooking surface made to be used outdoors. Think of it as an extra-large cast iron skillet. Most flat top griddles run on propane, but some newer models are electric. The cooking surfaces come in various sizes, ranging from 17 inches all the way up to 36 inches. (If you have a smaller griddle, you may have to cook some of these recipes in batches, but the results will still be amazing.) Blackstone is just one of many brands of flat top griddles. You can use the recipes in this book for any brand of griddle you have.

A Blackstone griddle's large cooking space and heat zones allow you to cook large quantities of food *and* a wide range of different foods all at once, saving you both time and a sink full of dishes. A griddle is perfect for cooking for a crowd, meal prepping, camping or tailgate cooking, or just cooking in your own backyard.

There are a few things you need to do before you begin using your Blackstone griddle, and the most important (after setting it up) is seasoning your griddle.

Seasoning Your Griddle

Seasoning is the key to a long-lasting griddle. It creates a black coating on the surface that keeps food from sticking, prevents scratching and rust, and adds flavor to every meal you make. Griddle seasoning is very simple and is accomplished in three easy steps. You will need some dish soap, good-quality paper towels, cooking oil, and tongs. A full tank of propane is recommended because the process takes over an hour. You can use any cooking oil: olive oil, vegetable oil, avocado oil, or Blackstone's griddle seasoning and conditioning oil.

Step 1: Washing the Surface

First, fill a small bowl with a drop of dish soap and some water. Dip a few paper towels into the soapy water and use them to thoroughly clean the griddle's surface. This will remove any dust or dirt that may have accumulated during shipping. To rinse, pour some clean water onto the griddle, wipe it clean with paper towels to remove any soapy residue, repeat a few times, and then dry completely.

Step 2: Blackening the Griddle

Turn all burners to high heat for 15 minutes. You will notice some spots on the flat top start to darken slightly. Add 2–3 tablespoons of oil, depending on the size of your griddle. Use tongs to hold a paper towel or two and spread the oil over the entire surface. Be sure to get the corners, edges, and outer edges of the griddle. The tongs will protect your hands; heat-resistant gloves are an added option. A very thin, smooth, and even layer of oil is key to keeping food from sticking and preventing chipping.

Sit back and relax as the griddle starts to blacken, which should take 10–15 minutes. This blackening process will create a good amount of smoke; this is normal and what you want to see.

Once the smoke stops, apply another very thin, smooth layer of oil, spreading it with the paper towel and tongs just like in the first step. Wait another 10–15 minutes. Then apply one last coat of oil, waiting 10–15 minutes before turning your Blackstone off.

Step 3: Final Coat of Oil

It is normal for the center of your griddle to be black, with the edges and corners a slightly lighter color. Not as much heat hits those areas, but after your first few cooks, the entire surface will become the same blackened color.

After your griddle cools slightly, apply just one more very thin layer of oil and use the tongs and paper towels to spread the oil evenly. Cover your griddle, and it will be ready to go for your first cook!

Tools for Your Griddle

You're almost ready to start cooking on your new griddle, but first, let's look at some tools and accessories. A few items are essential, and some will simply make your Blackstone griddle camping adventures easier and more comfortable. Here are the top tools and accessories to consider and the best uses for each.

Spatulas

Your most-used tool will probably be a set of two hibachi spatulas—long, narrow spatulas made of thin metal with handles. They are mostly used for stir-fries, fried rice, and flipping, and they can also be used for transferring food from the griddle. You can use both spatulas together to scoop stir-fries or use only one spatula for burgers. A friendly word of caution, though: It takes some practice to get the hang of using them. Just have fun with them, and after a few cooking sessions, you'll be a pro.

Tongs

Tongs are used for placing or flipping delicate food or items that don't have a flat surface—for example, kebabs, salmon, crostini, or some vegetables. You should invest in a longer pair of tongs, about 12 to 18 inches, to protect your hands from the flat top's heat while cooking and especially while seasoning your Blackstone.

Scraper

A griddle scraper is a thin, short piece of metal with a handle. Pretty much every time you use your griddle, you'll use this tool to push food particles to the grease cup to keep the griddle clean. Always remember to use the scraper gently to prevent scratching your griddle surface. You can also use the scraper to break up food, such as ground beef or chicken. Hold the scraper firmly and press down on the meat to chop or separate it as it cooks on the Blackstone.

Squeeze Bottles

It's handy to have at least two squeeze bottles at your outdoor cooking station: one with water and one with cooking oil. You will use both during every cook, so it's nice to have them ready to go. Choose good-quality plastic bottles. Lids on the caps are a bonus. Keep them away from the griddle flame so the plastic doesn't melt.

Melting Dome

Most camping griddle models come with a lid that lowers to keep the heat in. If your griddle doesn't have one, you'll need a melting dome. That's a metal dome a little over a foot wide, with a handle for easy lifting, used to melt cheese and steam vegetables.

Another option (and a good solution if what you want to cover is larger than your melting dome) is to use a disposable foil pan. Use caution with that, though; the pan may be extremely hot when it's time to remove it.

Burger Press

Another great tool for the Blackstone griddle is a small, round stainless steel burger press. Burger presses come in many varieties, but a stainless steel one is easier to clean and weighs less than a cast iron model. In addition to using your burger press to smash burgers, tacos, and potatoes, you can also use it to put pressure on or flatten bacon, wraps, and melted sandwiches.

Egg Rings

Egg rings are small, circular devices that keep food contained on the griddle. Metal egg rings can be used, but silicone rings are easier to clean and do a better job of keeping food in place. Besides their classic use (cooking eggs for breakfast sandwiches), these tools can also be used to make cakes, brownies, and corn bread. Buying a set of sixteen rings is a good idea if you plan to do a lot of cakes and brownies.

Camping Caddy

You may want to get a camping caddy with a handle to store and carry your camping cooking tools. That way, everything is in one place for convenience. In addition to holding your griddle tools and squirt bottles of water and oil, a caddy is also a great place to keep a roll of paper towels, a pepper grinder, kosher salt, and other seasoning blends that you use often.

Some other supplies to keep in your camping caddy to prepare the recipes in this book are a knife and cutting board, a small saucepan, a handheld can opener, and a medium-sized mixing bowl. It's also a good idea to have a few pairs of disposable rubber gloves, especially when handling raw meat, as handwashing at a campground is not always convenient.

Blackstone Griddle Camping Tips

The recipes in this book are designed specifically for camping, so many of them have fewer than five ingredients—and they all use ingredients that are easy to pack. Many of the recipes also use pre-packaged or store-bought ingredients for convenience, since resources are limited at the campsite. Here are a few other hints to help your first cook go as smoothly as possible.

- First, and most importantly, preparation is key to successful and stress-free griddle cooking. Have your ingredients chopped and measured and packages open because Blackstone cooking can go very quickly.
- When packing your cooler for camping, you should prepare and chop as many of your ingredients as possible and store them in gallon-sized plastic bags. If a recipe requires diced and marinated steak or chicken, prepare that at home and store it in a plastic bag in your cooler until ready to cook. Store-bought chopped vegetables, stir-fry kits, and prepared ingredients always help camp cooking go much more smoothly.
- Setting up a collapsible table at your campsite is great for food preparation. You can set out and organize all your ingredients on the table. Some griddles are even designed to sit on a table, making a very convenient camp cooking station.
- Remember to level your griddle! Campgrounds aren't always perfectly flat, and one of the most frustrating ways to figure that out is when all of your food is sliding across your Blackstone. Use a level or the Blackstone leveling shims under the griddle legs to keep the griddle from tilting—nobody wants grease pooling to one side of their griddle.
- Preheating your griddle for several minutes is important. It can take 3–4 minutes for the griddle to properly preheat.
- Know your griddle's hot spots and cooler areas. Typically, the center is the hottest and the edges are more on the warm side. Use those areas to your advantage by moving food around if something is cooking too quickly or not quickly enough.
- Outside temperatures can play a role in griddle surface temperatures. Adjust cooking times as needed based on the air temperature.
- You can cook an entire meal with multiple components on your Blackstone, but when you're first getting started with using it for camp cooking, keep things very simple. Begin with the easiest recipes and work your way up to becoming a griddle master!

Cleaning Your Blackstone Griddle

One of the best parts of griddle cooking is just how easy the cleanup is. It only takes three simple steps! Once you remove your food from your griddle, leave it on medium heat. The heat will make the cleaning process much easier and will prevent food particles from cooling and sticking. Most of the time, you can clean your griddle right away—it takes less than a minute. But you can certainly enjoy the delicious meal that you prepared first and save cleanup for later.

Step 1: Clear Food from the Surface

First, use a scraper to remove any food that is still on the surface. The level of scraping will be determined by what you cooked or by how much mess is left. If there are only a few crumbs, you'll just need to use a dry paper towel or griddle scraper to push them into the grease cup. If you have a small amount of food stuck to your griddle, you may need to scrape a little more. Gentle scraping is always key to protecting the surface.

For very messy situations, pour some water on your griddle and use the scraper to push everything into the grease cup. The water will help loosen any food or grease that has stuck. This is especially helpful when you've cooked with sticky or sweet sauces that may have burned onto the surface.

Step 2: Wipe the Surface Clean

Use a paper towel to dry and clean the surface. Be sure to get those corners and edges too. Use a good-quality brand of paper towels, or even heavy-duty blue shop towels, to prevent any lint from sticking to your griddle. Because the surface will still be hot, use tongs, not your hands, to hold the paper towels—or use your griddle scraper to push the paper towel around.

Step 3: Oil the Surface

The final step is applying a thin coat of oil. Drizzle some oil and use a dry paper towel to evenly spread it over the entire surface. You can use tongs or a griddle scraper to hold the paper towel as described in Step 2. The thin oil layer will help protect the griddle surface from rusting and ensure it stays well seasoned. A well-oiled griddle will also prevent food from sticking in the future.

Now that your griddle is clean and beautiful again, cover it back up, and it will be all ready to go for your next griddle cook!

BREAKFAST

There's no better way to start the day than with an energizing, hearty breakfast to prepare for your camping activities. In this chapter, you will find a variety of delicious and easy-to-make breakfasts that don't require a ton of ingredients or time. These recipes are not limited to just mornings though; remember, everyone loves a great breakfast-for-dinner as well! In the following pages, you will find fun and satisfying recipes like Waffle Breakfast Pizzas, Donut French Toast Sliders, Breakfast Grilled Cheeses, Avocado Hash Brown Toast, and Ham, Egg, and Cheese Muffins. These breakfasts not only taste great but are super quick to cook on the Blackstone griddle, so you will have plenty of time for all your camping fun!

BREAKFAST SLOPPY JOES

A breakfast version of a dinnertime classic! You can also make this dish spicy by using chorizo in place of the sausage and swapping out the Cheddar for pepper jack cheese. Be sure to grab some napkins for this one—it's sloppy.

PREP TIME MINUTES **5** ▲ COOK TIME MINUTES **10** ▲ SERVES **6**

- 6 large eggs
- 1⁄4 teaspoon kosher salt
- 1⁄8 teaspoon ground black pepper
- 1 pound ground breakfast sausage
- 1 cup shredded Cheddar cheese
- 1⁄4 cup pure maple syrup
- 6 brioche burger buns

1. Crack eggs into a medium bowl. Add salt and pepper, beat with a fork until combined, and set aside.
2. Preheat griddle to medium. Add sausage and cook 7 minutes, breaking meat apart with spatulas.
3. Slowly pour eggs over sausage and combine with spatulas, cooking and mixing 2 minutes.
4. Add cheese and syrup on top of sausage and eggs, use spatulas to mix together, and cook 1 more minute until cheese is melted. Serve on burger buns.

PER SERVING: Calories: 548 | Fat: 28g | Sodium: 1,052mg | Carbohydrates: 42g | Fiber: 1g | Sugar: 16g | Protein: 28g

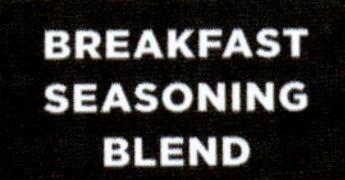

BREAKFAST SEASONING BLEND

Blackstone has a Lumber Jack breakfast seasoning blend that would be a great addition to this sandwich and many of the other breakfast recipes in this chapter. In fact, the recipes in this chapter were intentionally created to have minimal seasoning so you can add your own flair and personality with your favorite seasoning blends.

CHICKEN AND WAFFLE SANDWICHES

This handheld version of chicken and waffles is very convenient while camping. Feel free to add scrambled eggs and/or a slice of cheese to create a heartier breakfast sandwich.

PREP TIME MINUTES **10** ▲ COOK TIME MINUTES **8** ▲ SERVES **4**

- **8 frozen Eggo waffles, thawed**
- **4 frozen breaded chicken patties, thawed**
- **¼ cup pure maple syrup**

1. Preheat griddle to medium. Put waffles and chicken patties on griddle. Cook waffles 3–4 minutes, flipping both waffles and chicken a few times. Remove waffles once crisped to your liking.
2. Continue cooking chicken patties another 3–4 minutes, flipping a few times, until crisped to your liking.
3. To assemble sandwiches, drizzle half of the syrup on 4 of the waffles, place a chicken patty on top of each, drizzle remaining syrup on chicken, and add remaining 4 waffles. Serve.

PER SERVING: Calories: 445 | Fat: 20g | Sodium: 792mg | Carbohydrates: 51g | Fiber: 1g | Sugar: 14g | Protein: 15g

PATRIOTIC PANCAKES

Red, white, and blue pancakes are perfect for the Fourth of July. You could add red, white, and blue sprinkles to the pancake mix in place of the fruit and chocolate.

PREP TIME MINUTES **10** ▲ COOK TIME MINUTES **7** ▲ SERVES **4**

- **2 cups prepared pancake batter**
- **⅓ cup sliced strawberries**
- **⅓ cup blueberries**
- **⅓ cup white chocolate chips**
- **2 tablespoons unsalted butter**
- **⅓ cup pure maple syrup**

1. Place pancake batter in a medium bowl and gently stir strawberries, blueberries, and chocolate chips into the batter.
2. Preheat griddle to medium-low. Add butter and, once melted, spread evenly.
3. Spoon batter onto griddle to make 8 equal cakes. Cook 2–3 minutes per side. Serve with syrup drizzled over top.

PER SERVING: Calories: 386 | Fat: 12g | Sodium: 504mg | Carbohydrates: 63g | Fiber: 1g | Sugar: 33g | Protein: 5g

SCRAMBLED PANCAKES

This dish is not your traditional pancake breakfast—it is more reminiscent of scrambled eggs. Serve these pancakes with a side of bacon or sausage for a complete, hearty meal.

PREP TIME MINUTES **5** ▲ COOK TIME MINUTES **5** ▲ SERVES **4**

- **2 tablespoons unsalted butter**
- **2 cups prepared pancake batter**
- **½ cup pure maple syrup**

1. Preheat griddle to medium-low. Add butter and, once melted, pour all the pancake batter on griddle.
2. Use your spatulas to mix batter like you would scramble eggs. Cook and scramble 3–4 minutes until batter is cooked through. Serve with maple syrup drizzled over top.

PER SERVING: Calories: 333 | Fat: 8g | Sodium: 492mg | Carbohydrates: 61g | Fiber: 1g | Sugar: 31g | Protein: 4g

AVOCADO HASH BROWN TOAST

Avocado toast gets a fun twist in this breakfast dish. You can use prepared mashed avocado for convenience rather than having to mash a fresh avocado at the campsite.

PREP TIME MINUTES **10** ▲ COOK TIME MINUTES **12** ▲ SERVES **4**

- **2 tablespoons unsalted butter, divided**
- **4 frozen hash brown patties, thawed**
- **4 large eggs**
- **1 large avocado, peeled, pitted, and mashed**
- **1 teaspoon Everything Bagel seasoning**

1. Preheat griddle to medium. Add 1 tablespoon butter and, once melted, place hash browns on griddle. Cook 8 minutes, flipping halfway through the cooking time. Remove once golden brown and crisp and set aside.
2. Place four silicone egg rings on griddle. Cut remaining 1 tablespoon butter into four equal pieces and place one butter piece into each egg ring. Crack eggs into rings and cook 2 minutes, then remove egg rings and flip eggs. Cook 1 more minute and remove when eggs are cooked to your liking.
3. Spread mashed avocado on top of hash browns, top each with a fried egg, and sprinkle seasoning over top. Serve.

PER SERVING: Calories: 304 | Fat: 20g | Sodium: 394mg | Carbohydrates: 17g | Fiber: 4g | Sugar: 0g | Protein: 8g

HOT MESS BREAKFAST EXPRESS

This dish features all your breakfast favorites scrambled into a delicious mess. This is often known as a "Mountain Man Breakfast," but this recipe uses the griddle instead of the traditional Dutch oven. Hot sauce is a great addition to this breakfast.

PREP TIME MINUTES **5** ▲ COOK TIME MINUTES **22** ▲ SERVES **8**

- **1 pound ground breakfast sausage**
- **4 tablespoons unsalted butter**
- **15 ounces frozen shredded hash browns, thawed**
- **1 teaspoon kosher salt**
- **½ teaspoon ground black pepper**
- **6 large eggs**
- **2 cups shredded Cheddar cheese, divided**
- **½ cup sour cream**

1. Preheat griddle to medium. Add sausage and cook 7 minutes, breaking meat apart with spatulas.
2. Put butter on top of sausage and, once melted, spread evenly, then sprinkle hash browns, salt, and pepper over top. Cook 10 minutes, mixing and flipping a few times. Press spatulas into hash browns to brown and crisp them.
3. Crack eggs over hash browns–sausage mixture. Use spatulas to break them apart and scramble everything together for 3 minutes.
4. Sprinkle 1 cup cheese over mixture, using spatulas to mix together. Sprinkle remaining 1 cup cheese over mixture and, without mixing, lower griddle lid or use melting dome for 1 minute until cheese is melted.
5. Serve in bowls with dollops of sour cream on top.

PER SERVING: Calories: 437 | Fat: 31g | Sodium: 914mg | Carbohydrates: 11g | Fiber: 1g | Sugar: 1g | Protein: 21g

EGG AND SAUSAGE GRAVY BURRITOS

Biscuits and sausage gravy were the inspiration behind these breakfast burritos. This recipe uses canned sausage gravy to make a quick and easy meal before a day of fun at the campground.

PREP TIME MINUTES **10** ▲ COOK TIME MINUTES **9** ▲ SERVES **8**

6 large eggs

¼ teaspoon kosher salt

⅛ teaspoon ground black pepper

2 tablespoons unsalted butter, divided

1 cup shredded Cheddar cheese

8 (8-inch) soft flour tortillas

1 (15-ounce) can sausage gravy

1. Crack eggs into a medium bowl. Add salt and pepper and beat with a fork until combined.
2. Preheat griddle to medium. Add 1 tablespoon butter and, once melted, slowly pour eggs onto griddle. Cook 2 minutes, mixing and scrambling with spatulas.
3. Sprinkle cheese over top and mix 1 more minute until cheese is melted. Remove from griddle.
4. Place tortillas on griddle for 30 seconds to warm them; this makes them more pliable. Remove tortillas from griddle.
5. On a work surface, assemble burritos by spreading sausage gravy in the center of each tortilla. Place egg-and-cheese mixture over top of gravy. Fold in the sides of each tortilla and tightly roll into burritos.
6. Add remaining 1 tablespoon butter to griddle and, once melted, place burritos seam-side down on griddle. Cook 1–2 minutes per side until golden brown and crisped to your liking. Let cool slightly before serving.

PER SERVING: Calories: 332 | Fat: 17g | Sodium: 785mg | Carbohydrates: 28g | Fiber: 1g | Sugar: 2g | Protein: 13g

WAFFLE BREAKFAST PIZZAS

Pizza for breakfast is always a fun option, especially when waffles are the crust. You can make these your own by adding any toppings of your choice.

PREP TIME MINUTES **10** ▲ COOK TIME MINUTES **16** ▲ SERVES **6**

- **4 slices bacon**
- **4 large eggs**
- **¼ teaspoon kosher salt**
- **⅛ teaspoon ground black pepper**
- **1 tablespoon unsalted butter**
- **¾ cup diced deli ham**
- **6 frozen Eggo waffles, thawed**
- **¼ cup pure maple syrup**
- **1 cup shredded Cheddar cheese**

1. Preheat griddle to medium-low. Place bacon slices on griddle and cook 5–7 minutes, flipping a few times, until bacon is cooked to your liking. Remove from griddle, set aside, and scrape grease into grease cup.
2. Crack eggs into a medium bowl. Add salt and pepper and beat with a fork until combined.
3. Raise griddle to medium heat. Add butter and, once melted, add ham. Slowly pour eggs over ham. Mix and scramble with spatulas 2–3 minutes until eggs are set. Remove from griddle.
4. Put waffles on griddle and cook 3–4 minutes, flipping a few times, until crisped to your liking.
5. Drizzle syrup over each waffle, spoon on ham-and-egg mixture, and sprinkle cheese over top. Lower griddle lid or use melting dome for 1 minute until cheese is melted.
6. Crumble bacon over top and serve.

PER SERVING: Calories: 333 | Fat: 17g | Sodium: 866mg | Carbohydrates: 23g | Fiber: 0g | Sugar: 9g | Protein: 18g

NUTELLA-STUFFED FRENCH TOAST

The only thing better than French toast at the campground is stuffed French toast, of course! Use disposable rubber gloves when dipping the French toast for easier cleanup.

PREP TIME MINUTES **10** ▲ COOK TIME MINUTES **7** ▲ SERVES **4**

- **4 ounces Nutella**
- **8 (1-inch) slices brioche**
- **2 large eggs**
- **¼ cup 2% milk**
- **1 tablespoon granulated sugar**
- **2 tablespoons unsalted butter**
- **1 tablespoon confectioners' sugar**

1. Spread Nutella onto 4 slices of bread. Top each with another slice of bread, pressing together slightly.
2. Crack eggs into a medium bowl. Add milk and sugar and beat with a fork until combined.
3. Preheat griddle to medium-low. Add butter and, once melted, dip each sandwich into the egg mixture on both sides for 10 seconds. Place on griddle and cook 2–3 minutes per side until golden brown.
4. Serve with confectioners' sugar sprinkled over top.

PER SERVING: Calories: 451 | Fat: 17g | Sodium: 399mg | Carbohydrates: 65g | Fiber: 1g | Sugar: 27g | Protein: 9g

You could add sliced bananas or strawberries to the center of each sandwich right on top of the Nutella before adding the top slice of bread. Or use whipped cream cheese and your fruit of choice in place of the Nutella filling. You can even create a sweet and savory version by adding two slices of bacon to the Nutella filling. In place of the confectioners' sugar, you could top your French toast with whipped cream.

HUEVOS RANCHEROS STIR-FRY

Huevos rancheros is typically served with beans on a crispy fried corn tortilla topped with a fried egg. This is an easy mixed-up version of that classic dish using tortilla chips. Feel free to add sour cream, hot sauce, or avocado as optional toppings.

PREP TIME MINUTES **5** ▲ COOK TIME MINUTES **6** ▲ SERVES **4**

- 8 ounces corn tortilla chips
- 1 (15-ounce) can black beans, drained but not rinsed
- 1 cup salsa
- 4 large eggs
- ¼ teaspoon kosher salt
- 1 cup shredded Cheddar cheese

1. Preheat griddle to medium. Add tortilla chips, black beans, and salsa. Cook 2 minutes, mixing together with spatulas.
2. Crack eggs over top, add salt, and mix together, breaking eggs apart while cooking for another 3 minutes until eggs are cooked to your liking. Try to keep tortilla chips whole, but it's normal for some to break apart as they soften.
3. Sprinkle cheese over top and cook 1 more minute. Lower griddle lid or cover with melting dome to melt cheese. Serve on plates with forks.

PER SERVING: Calories: 579 | Fat: 24g | Sodium: 1,283mg | Carbohydrates: 60g | Fiber: 12g | Sugar: 5g | Protein: 23g

SMASHED CINNAMON ROLLS WITH BACON

These cinnamon rolls are best enjoyed when you eat them like pancakes, with a knife and fork. This dish combines a nice mix of sweet and savory flavors to start your day of camping off right.

PREP TIME MINUTES **10** ▲ COOK TIME MINUTES **11** ▲ SERVES **5**

5 slices bacon

1 (17.5-ounce, 5-count) tube jumbo cinnamon rolls with icing

1. Preheat griddle to medium-low. Place bacon slices on griddle and cook 5–7 minutes, flipping a few times, until bacon is cooked to your liking. Remove from griddle, set aside, and scrape grease into grease cup.
2. Place cinnamon rolls on griddle spaced 4 inches apart. Use a burger press to smash them as flat as possible. Cook 2 minutes, flip, and smash them again. Cook 2 more minutes or until dough is cooked through.
3. Remove cinnamon rolls from griddle, spread icing from package onto each one, and crumble a slice of bacon over each. Serve.

PER SERVING: Calories: 413 | Fat: 20g | Sodium: 723mg | Carbohydrates: 49g | Fiber: 1g | Sugar: 20g | Protein: 8g

In place of the bacon, you can top your smashed cinnamon rolls with fresh berries or a can of apple pie filling. Of course, you should still drizzle the icing over the top. For added crunch, try sprinkling the rolls with some Fruity Pebbles cereal.

DONUT FRENCH TOAST SLIDERS

This creative combo of donuts, French toast, and sausage breakfast sandwiches is a camping breakfast the kids are sure to love.

PREP TIME MINUTES **10** ▲ COOK TIME MINUTES **15** ▲ SERVES **4**

- 8 glazed donuts
- 2 large eggs
- ¼ cup 2% milk
- 4 (2-ounce) sausage patties
- 1 tablespoon unsalted butter

1. On your workspace, use a burger press to smash donuts flat. Crack eggs into a medium bowl, add milk, and beat with a fork until combined.
2. Preheat griddle to medium. Add sausage patties and cook 3–4 minutes per side; remove from griddle once cooked through. Lower heat to medium-low.
3. Add butter to griddle and, once melted, dip each donut into egg mixture for 10 seconds and place donuts on griddle. Cook 2–3 minutes per side.
4. Place a sausage patty on each of 4 donuts and then top with 4 remaining donuts. Serve.

PER SERVING: Calories: 576 | Fat: 37g | Sodium: 712mg | Carbohydrates: 42g | Fiber: 0g | Sugar: 19g | Protein: 16g

BREAKFAST GRILLED CHEESES

This recipe combines two childhood favorites—egg in a hole and the traditional grilled cheese—to create the ultimate breakfast grilled cheese sandwiches.

PREP TIME MINUTES **10** ▲ COOK TIME MINUTES **7** ▲ SERVES **4**

- **4 (1-ounce) slices American cheese**
- **8 slices white sandwich bread**
- **2 tablespoons unsalted butter**
- **4 large eggs**
- **¼ teaspoon kosher salt**
- **⅛ teaspoon ground black pepper**

1. Place 1 slice of cheese each on 4 slices of bread and then top each with remaining 4 bread slices. Use a 2-inch biscuit cutter, lid, or top of a cup to cut a circle out of the center of each; remove the circle.
2. Preheat griddle to medium-low. Add butter and, once melted, add sandwiches and bread circles with cheese.
3. Crack an egg into the empty circle of each sandwich and sprinkle salt and pepper over eggs. Cook 2–3 minutes per side, flipping both sandwiches and cheesy circles.
4. Remove once bread is golden brown, cheese is melted, and eggs are cooked how you like them. Let cool slightly before serving.

PER SERVING: Calories: 349 | Fat: 15g | Sodium: 1,107mg | Carbohydrates: 33g | Fiber: 2g | Sugar: 6g | Protein: 16g

HAM, EGG, AND CHEESE MUFFINS

These easy and portable English muffin sandwiches are similar to a breakfast sandwich at your favorite fast-food restaurant, but they are so much better for you. Feel free to use Canadian bacon or sausage patties in place of the ham.

PREP TIME MINUTES **5** ▲ COOK TIME MINUTES **6** ▲ SERVES **4**

1 tablespoon unsalted butter, cut into fourths

4 large eggs

¼ teaspoon kosher salt

4 (1-ounce) slices deli ham

4 (1-ounce) slices American cheese

4 English muffins, sliced

1. Preheat griddle to medium. Place four silicone egg rings on griddle and a piece of butter into each ring. Crack an egg into each ring and sprinkle salt over top. Cook 1–2 minutes, remove egg rings and flip eggs. Cook 1 more minute or until eggs are cooked to your liking. Remove eggs and set aside.
2. Place ham slices on griddle spaced 1 inch apart, folding if needed to make slices about the same size as English muffins. Cook 1 minute, flip, and then place a slice of cheese over each ham slice. Allow to melt 1 minute.
3. On an empty side of the griddle, place English muffins, cut side down, and cook 30 seconds to warm them.
4. To assemble, place ham and cheese on each bottom English muffin slice, top with egg, and add top English muffin slice. Serve.

PER SERVING: Calories: 323 | Fat: 13g | Sodium: 1,075mg | Carbohydrates: 29g | Fiber: 2g | Sugar: 5g | Protein: 21g

MINI DONUT DIPPERS

These bite-sized cinnamon-sugar donuts are dipped in chocolate sauce for the ultimate camping breakfast treat. You could also dip these in your favorite warm fruit preserves to make them more like jelly donuts.

PREP TIME MINUTES **5** ▲ COOK TIME MINUTES **10** ▲ SERVES **4**

- **1 (7.5-ounce, 10-count) tube refrigerated biscuit dough**
- **¼ cup granulated sugar**
- **2 teaspoons ground cinnamon**
- **3 tablespoons unsalted butter, divided**
- **¼ cup chocolate sauce**

1. Cut each biscuit into fourths. Put sugar and cinnamon in a medium bowl and stir until combined.
2. Preheat griddle to medium-low. Add 1 tablespoon butter and, once melted, place biscuit pieces on griddle. Cook 7–8 minutes, flipping a few times with tongs, until golden brown. Add remaining 2 tablespoons butter and toss with spatulas until biscuits are coated.
3. Transfer biscuit pieces to bowl with cinnamon-sugar mixture and toss until coated. Serve with chocolate sauce for dipping.

PER SERVING: Calories: 306 | Fat: 8g | Sodium: 520mg | Carbohydrates: 51g | Fiber: 2g | Sugar: 21g | Protein: 4g

SNACKS AND SIDES

In this chapter, you will find a variety of side dishes to accompany almost any main dish, plus an array of snacks to enjoy any time of day. There are also a few appetizer ideas for when you are invited to a friend's campsite for a night of fun or when you just feel like enjoying a "snacky dinner night" around the campfire after a long day. Here you will find dishes like Caprese Brie and Crostini, Caribbean Jerk Chicken Dip, BBQ Pork Nachos, Parmesan Bacon and Corn, Biscuits with Honey Butter, and Cheesy Mashed Potato Cakes. With so many delicious options to choose from, you may have trouble deciding which one to cook first!

SPINACH AND ARTICHOKE FLATBREAD

These flatbreads make a quick and easy camping snack or a lighter meal on the Blackstone. You can also try creating another variation of this dish by using store-bought buffalo chicken dip and Cheddar.

PREP TIME MINUTES **5** ▲ COOK TIME MINUTES **6** ▲ SERVES **4**

- **2 (4-ounce) naan flatbreads**
- **1 (8-ounce) container store-bought spinach and artichoke dip**
- **1 cup shredded mozzarella cheese**

1. Preheat griddle to medium-low. Put naan flatbreads on griddle 1 minute and then flip. Evenly spread dip onto flatbreads and sprinkle cheese over top.
2. Lower griddle lid or cover with melting dome 3–5 minutes until cheese is melted
3. Slice into smaller pieces and serve warm.

PER SERVING: Calories: 327 | Fat: 16g | Sodium: 975mg | Carbohydrates: 31g | Fiber: 1g | Sugar: 3g | Protein: 14g

PIGS IN A BLANKET

Here is a classic snack that kids love made on the Blackstone—and it brings a little nostalgia for the adults too. Set out both ketchup and mustard for dipping.

PREP TIME MINUTES **10** ▲ COOK TIME MINUTES **17** ▲ SERVES **6**

1 (8-ounce, 8-count) tube crescent rolls

24 Lit'l Smokies sausages

2 tablespoons unsalted butter

1. Separate the triangle pieces of crescent dough and cut each triangle into thirds. Roll the crescent dough pieces around each sausage, stretching the dough as needed.
2. Preheat griddle to low. Add butter and, once melted, place the Pigs in a Blanket on the griddle. Cover with griddle lid or melting dome and cook 14–16 minutes total, flipping a few times with tongs. Cover with lid or melting dome each time after flipping.
3. Remove once dough is golden brown and cooked through. Serve.

PER SERVING: Calories: 304 | Fat: 22g | Sodium: 643mg | Carbohydrates: 18g | Fiber: 0g | Sugar: 4g | Protein: 8g

CAPRESE BRIE AND CROSTINI

This loaded, melty cheese dish with a side of toasted bread is more of a "glamping" type of snack. In reality, it is quick to prepare but is sure to impress your friends and family!

PREP TIME MINUTES **10** ▲ COOK TIME MINUTES **10** ▲ SERVES **5**

- 3 tablespoons olive oil, divided
- 1 pint whole grape tomatoes
- ½ teaspoon kosher salt, divided
- ¼ teaspoon ground black pepper, divided
- 1 (8-ounce) package Brie
- 2 ounces pesto
- 1 (16-ounce) loaf French bread, cut into 20 slices
- 2 ounces balsamic glaze

1. Preheat griddle to medium. Add 1 tablespoon oil, tomatoes, ¼ teaspoon salt, and ⅛ teaspoon pepper to one side of the griddle. On the other side, place Brie on parchment paper or a heat-proof plate and cover with melting dome. Cook 6–7 minutes, mixing tomatoes with spatulas, until tomatoes are soft and slightly charred.
2. Remove Brie from griddle and place on a tray or cutting board. Spread pesto on top of Brie and place tomatoes over top.
3. Add remaining 2 tablespoons oil to griddle and then slices of bread. Season with remaining ¼ teaspoon salt and remaining ⅛ teaspoon pepper. Cook 1 minute per side or until crisped to your liking.
4. Drizzle balsamic glaze over Brie. Arrange crostini slices around the tray or cutting board and serve with a knife to spread warm Brie and toppings on crostini.

PER SERVING: Calories: 531 | Fat: 22g | Sodium: 1,139mg | Carbohydrates: 61g | Fiber: 3g | Sugar: 17g | Protein: 20g

In place of the Brie, you could serve the tomatoes, pesto, and balsamic glaze over 8 ounces of sliced fresh mozzarella cheese at room temperature. This is excellent with the crostini or on a bed of arugula for a fresh salad option.

LOADED POTATO PATTIES

This camping version of potato skins makes the perfect late-night snack around the campfire, or you can serve these as a side dish for steak or burgers.

PREP TIME MINUTES **5** ▲ COOK TIME MINUTES **16** ▲ SERVES **4**

4 slices bacon

8 frozen hash brown patties, thawed

1½ cups shredded Cheddar cheese

½ cup sour cream

1. Preheat griddle to medium-low. Add bacon and cook 5–7 minutes, flipping a few times. Remove once cooked to your liking. Raise heat to medium.
2. Place hash browns on griddle on top of bacon grease. Cook 8 minutes, flipping a few times, until crisped and golden brown.
3. Top each patty evenly with cheese and crumble bacon over top. Lower griddle lid or cover with melting dome 1 minute until cheese is melted.
4. Serve with a dollop of sour cream on top of each patty.

PER SERVING: Calories: 521 | Fat: 33g | Sodium: 959mg | Carbohydrates: 30g | Fiber: 4g | Sugar: 1g | Protein: 17g

GARLIC HERB TOMATOES

This simple side dish is especially delicious in the summer when tomatoes are in season. Feel free to use any kind of tomato you like and fresh herbs if you have them.

PREP TIME MINUTES **10** ▲ COOK TIME MINUTES **4** ▲ SERVES **4**

2 tablespoons olive oil

4 medium Roma tomatoes, ends removed and cut into ½-inch rounds

¼ teaspoon kosher salt, divided

⅛ teaspoon ground black pepper, divided

½ teaspoon Italian seasoning blend, divided

¼ teaspoon garlic powder, divided

¼ cup grated Parmesan cheese

1. Preheat griddle to medium. Add oil and tomatoes, season with ⅛ teaspoon salt, 1⁄16 teaspoon pepper, ¼ teaspoon Italian seasoning, and ⅛ teaspoon garlic powder. Cook 2 minutes.
2. Flip and season with remaining ⅛ teaspoon salt, 1⁄16 teaspoon pepper, ¼ teaspoon Italian seasoning, and ⅛ teaspoon garlic powder. Sprinkle Parmesan over top. Cook 1–2 more minutes until tomatoes are charred to your liking.
3. Let cool slightly before serving.

PER SERVING: Calories: 82 | Fat: 6g | Sodium: 209mg | Carbohydrates: 4g | Fiber: 1g | Sugar: 2g | Protein: 3g

CHORIZO AND CORN NACHOS

These nachos can be a late-night snack or even a fun dinner because there are no rules when it comes to meals at the campsite. Add toppings such as jalapeños, salsa, shredded lettuce, or pickled red onions if you'd like.

PREP TIME MINUTES **10** ▲ COOK TIME MINUTES **12** ▲ SERVES **8**

1 pound ground chorizo

1 (15-ounce) can corn, drained

1 (13-ounce) bag corn tortilla chips

4 cups shredded Monterey jack cheese

1 (15-ounce) jar queso blanco

1 cup sour cream

1. Preheat griddle to medium. Add chorizo and cook 5 minutes, breaking meat apart with spatulas.
2. Add corn and cook 2 more minutes, mixing. Remove from griddle and lower heat to medium-low.
3. Spread tortilla chips in a single layer on griddle, overlapping slightly. Sprinkle half of cheese, half of chorizo-corn mixture, queso, remaining half of cheese, and then remaining chorizo-corn mixture over chips.
4. Lower griddle lid or cover with melting dome 5 minutes or until cheese is melted.
5. Drizzle or dollop sour cream over top before serving.

PER SERVING: Calories: 736 | Fat: 48g | Sodium: 1,418mg | Carbohydrates: 43g | Fiber: 3g | Sugar: 4g | Protein: 27g

HOECAKES

Hoecakes, also called johnnycakes, are fried corn cakes or savory cornmeal pancakes. They make a simple but delicious side dish for any meal at the campsite. You can top these with butter or jelly or enjoy them plain.

PREP TIME MINUTES **10** ▲ COOK TIME MINUTES **7** ▲ SERVES **8**

- 2 (8.5-ounce) boxes Jiffy Corn Muffin Mix
- 1 cup plus 2 tablespoons 2% buttermilk
- 1 large egg
- 2 tablespoons unsalted butter

1. In a medium bowl, add corn muffin mix, buttermilk, and egg. Stir until combined.
2. Preheat griddle to medium. Add butter and, once melted, spoon batter onto griddle to make 8 equal cakes.
3. Cook 2–3 minutes per side or until edges are crisped and cakes are golden brown.
4. Serve while still warm.

PER SERVING: Calories: 301 | Fat: 11g | Sodium: 613mg | Carbohydrates: 45g | Fiber: 0g | Sugar: 13g | Protein: 5g

SILICONE EGGS RINGS

If you want your Hoecakes to be cooked in perfect circles, you could use silicone egg rings. Place the egg rings on the Blackstone and add a pat of butter to each. Pour batter into the rings, then remove rings after 2–3 minutes. Flip cakes and set egg rings aside. This makes for a nice presentation.

HERB PITA CHIPS WITH HUMMUS

These chips and hummus make a great light snack or even a side dish with dinner. The pita chips get slightly crisp on the outside but remain soft on the inside.

PREP TIME MINUTES **10** ▲ COOK TIME MINUTES **6** ▲ SERVES **4**

2 tablespoons unsalted butter, at room temperature

4 pieces pita bread

1 teaspoon garlic powder

1 teaspoon dried oregano

¼ teaspoon kosher salt

1 cup hummus

1. Use a butter knife to spread butter on both sides of each pita bread. Sprinkle garlic powder, oregano, and salt on both sides.
2. Preheat griddle to medium. Place pita breads on griddle and cook 2–3 minutes per side until crisped to your liking. Press slightly with spatulas or use a burger press to flatten the pitas as they cook.
3. Let cool slightly. Slice each pita into 6 chips and serve with hummus for dipping.

PER SERVING: Calories: 320 | Fat: 11g | Sodium: 675mg | Carbohydrates: 43g | Fiber: 5g | Sugar: 1g | Protein: 11g

LEMON PEPPER CHICKEN WINGS

Chicken wings on the Blackstone achieve crispy skin with a tender, juicy bite every time. You can change up this recipe with any seasoning blend or wing sauce you like.

PREP TIME MINUTES **5** ▲ COOK TIME MINUTES **21** ▲ SERVES **6**

3 pounds jumbo, split chicken wings

1½ tablespoons lemon pepper seasoning blend

½ teaspoon kosher salt

¼ teaspoon ground black pepper

3 tablespoons vegetable oil

1. Season chicken wings with seasoning blend, salt, and pepper.
2. Preheat griddle to medium-high. Add oil and then chicken wings. Cook 3 minutes per side, using tongs to flip wings.
3. Lower heat to medium-low. Lower griddle lid or cover with melting dome. Cook 12–15 more minutes, removing the dome or lid a few times to flip wings. Remove once chicken is cooked through and skin is crisped to your liking.
4. Let cool slightly before serving.

PER SERVING: Calories: 472 | Fat: 33g | Sodium: 412mg | Carbohydrates: 0g | Fiber: 0g | Sugar: 0g | Protein: 40g

WONTON CHEESE STICKS

This recipe creates an extra-crispy version of a mozzarella cheese stick made on the Blackstone for a tasty snack. The result is a golden-brown shell filled with ooey-gooey, melty cheese.

PREP TIME MINUTES **10** ▲ COOK TIME MINUTES **5** ▲ SERVES **4**

4 mozzarella cheese sticks

12 wonton wrappers

3 tablespoons vegetable oil

½ cup pizza sauce

1. Cut each cheese stick into thirds. Lay wonton wrappers flat, with a corner facing you, and place a third of a cheese stick in the center of each. Dip your finger in water and trace around the edge of each wonton.
2. Fold side corners in over cheese, fold the top corner over cheese, and roll closed. Press seams to ensure they are closed. They should resemble mini egg rolls.
3. Preheat griddle to medium. Add oil and place cheese wontons on griddle. Cook 4–5 minutes total, turning several times with tongs.
4. Remove once wontons are crispy and golden brown. Let cool slightly before serving with pizza sauce for dipping.

PER SERVING: Calories: 234 | Fat: 14g | Sodium: 421mg | Carbohydrates: 17g | Fiber: 1g | Sugar: 1g | Protein: 9g

All Blackstone griddles have slightly varying surface temperatures based on the model, and outside temperature—a factor when cooking at a campsite—plays a part as well. In general, if your food doesn't seem to be cooking fast enough, try raising the heat slightly. And if it's cooking too quickly, try lowering the heat a bit.

CARIBBEAN JERK CHICKEN DIP

Once you master this dip, try using other flavors, such as barbecue sauce or your favorite wing sauce, in place of the Caribbean jerk sauce. Serve this with Fritos Scoops! or tortilla chips for dipping.

PREP TIME MINUTES **10** ▲ COOK TIME MINUTES **18** ▲ SERVES **8**

- **1 pound thin-cut, boneless, skinless chicken breasts**
- **½ teaspoon kosher salt**
- **¼ teaspoon ground black pepper**
- **1 tablespoon olive oil**
- **8 ounces Caribbean jerk sauce or marinade**
- **8 ounces cream cheese**
- **8 ounces ranch dressing**
- **2 cups shredded Monterey jack cheese**

1. Season chicken on both sides with salt and pepper.
2. Preheat griddle to medium. Add oil and then chicken. Cook chicken 4 minutes per side, remove once cooked through, and dice into bite-sized pieces.
3. Place a 9" × 13" foil pan on griddle, still over medium heat. Add cooked chicken, Caribbean jerk sauce, cream cheese, ranch, and cheese to the pan. Lower lid or cover with melting dome 9–10 minutes, stirring several times with a spoon. Serve once cheese is melted and everything is combined.

PER SERVING: Calories: 334 | Fat: 23g | Sodium: 1,216mg | Carbohydrates: 12g | Fiber: 0g | Sugar: 8g | Protein: 20g

BBQ PORK NACHOS

This is possibly one of the easiest nacho recipes around because of store-bought barbecue pork—it's the perfect snack for camping. You can even substitute barbecue chicken if desired. Drizzle barbecue sauce on top if you like things extra saucy.

PREP TIME MINUTES **10** ▲ COOK TIME MINUTES **5** ▲ SERVES **8**

1 (13-ounce) bag corn tortilla chips

4 cups shredded Monterey jack cheese

1 (16-ounce) container barbecue pulled pork at room temperature

1 (15-ounce) jar queso blanco

1 tablespoon barbecue seasoning blend

1 (4-ounce) can diced jalapeños, drained

8 ounces sour cream

1. Preheat griddle to medium-low. Spread tortilla chips evenly on griddle, overlapping slightly.
2. Sprinkle half of cheese, half of pork, jar of queso, remaining cheese, remaining pork, and barbecue seasoning evenly over chips.
3. Sprinkle jalapeños over top and lower griddle lid or cover with melting dome 5 minutes or until cheese is melted and pork is warmed through.
4. Drizzle or dollop sour cream over top before serving.

PER SERVING: Calories: 660 | Fat: 37g | Sodium: 1,362mg | Carbohydrates: 49g | Fiber: 3g | Sugar: 11g | Protein: 25g

BISCUITS WITH HONEY BUTTER

The honey butter really takes these simple biscuits up a notch. This is such an easy and delicious side dish to add to your camping meals.

PREP TIME MINUTES **10** ▲ COOK TIME MINUTES **9** ▲ SERVES **5**

1 (7.5-ounce, 10-count) tube refrigerated biscuit dough

5 tablespoons unsalted butter, at room temperature

2 tablespoons honey

¼ teaspoon ground cinnamon

1. Preheat griddle to medium-low. Place biscuits on griddle and cook 7–9 minutes, flipping with spatulas a few times.
2. While biscuits are cooking, add butter, honey, and cinnamon to a small bowl. Stir until combined.
3. When biscuits are golden brown and cooked through, spoon a small dollop of butter on each biscuit to melt over the top.
4. Serve biscuits with remaining honey butter.

PER SERVING: Calories: 227 | Fat: 11g | Sodium: 364mg | Carbohydrates: 27g | Fiber: 1g | Sugar: 9g | Protein: 3g

CHEESY PESTO BREADSTICKS

These breadsticks make a nice side dish by themselves, or you can serve them as a snack with a side of pizza sauce or pesto for dipping. Kids always go crazy over this recipe.

PREP TIME MINUTES **5** ▲ COOK TIME MINUTES **6** ▲ SERVES **6**

2 (4-ounce) naan flatbreads

4 ounces pesto

2 cups Italian blend shredded cheese

1. Preheat griddle to medium-low. Place naan flatbreads on griddle 1 minute and then flip.
2. Spread pesto evenly on each flatbread and sprinkle cheese over top. Lower griddle lid or cover with melting dome 3–5 minutes until cheese is melted.
3. Remove and cut each flatbread into 6 strips before serving.

PER SERVING: Calories: 296 | Fat: 17g | Sodium: 739mg | Carbohydrates: 22g | Fiber: 1g | Sugar: 2g | Protein: 14g

PARMESAN BACON AND CORN

This simplified version of skillet corn with bacon is perfect for Blackstone griddle cooking at the campground.

PREP TIME MINUTES **5** ▲ COOK TIME MINUTES **13** ▲ SERVES **4**

4 slices bacon

1 (12-ounce) bag frozen sweet corn, thawed

¼ teaspoon kosher salt

⅛ teaspoon ground black pepper

½ cup shredded Parmesan cheese

1. Preheat griddle to medium-low. Add bacon and cook 5–7 minutes, flipping a few times, until crisped to your liking. Remove bacon but leave grease on griddle.
2. Put corn on griddle with salt and pepper and cook 3–4 minutes, mixing with spatulas.
3. Add Parmesan and crumble cooked bacon over top. Cook 2 more minutes, mixing with spatulas. Serve warm.

PER SERVING: Calories: 170 | Fat: 7g | Sodium: 485mg | Carbohydrates: 18g | Fiber: 2g | Sugar: 2g | Protein: 10g

RANCH CHEX MIX

This snack mix is so deliciously addicting. This recipe makes a ton, but you can easily store any leftovers in plastic bags or sealed containers for a handy snack to enjoy on a hike or whenever you like.

PREP TIME MINUTES **5** ▲ COOK TIME MINUTES **10** ▲ SERVES **10**

2 cups Corn Chex

2 cups Wheat Chex

2 cups mini pretzels

2 cups Cheddar cheese crackers

1 cup salted peanuts

6 tablespoons unsalted butter, sliced into 6 slices

2 tablespoons Worcestershire sauce

2 tablespoons dry ranch seasoning

1. Preheat griddle to medium-low. Add both kinds of Chex, pretzels, cheese crackers, and peanuts.
2. Evenly add butter slices and Worcestershire sauce over top.
3. Use spatulas to gently mix and combine for 6 minutes, coating mixture evenly with butter. Sprinkle ranch seasoning over top and continue mixing 4 more minutes.
4. Remove mix and let cool slightly before serving.

PER SERVING: Calories: 333 | Fat: 16g | Sodium: 649mg | Carbohydrates: 39g | Fiber: 4g | Sugar: 3g | Protein: 9g

CHEX MIX TIPS

To avoid packing everything separately, try combining all the dry ingredients (minus the dry ranch seasoning) in either a large plastic storage bag or a sealed container. When it is time to make this recipe at the campground, it comes together very quickly. Feel free to stir in a sweet treat like M&M's or chocolate chips once the mixture has cooled.

MINI ZUCCHINI PIZZA ROUNDS

These zucchini rounds are like a low-carb version of pizza rolls. Omit the pepperoni for a vegetarian version or add any other pizza toppings you like.

PREP TIME MINUTES **10** ▲ COOK TIME MINUTES **4** ▲ SERVES **6**

- 2 tablespoons olive oil
- 2 medium zucchini, ends removed and sliced into 24 (½-inch-thick) rounds
- ½ teaspoon kosher salt
- ⅓ cup pizza sauce
- 1½ cups shredded mozzarella cheese
- 24 slices pepperoni
- ½ teaspoon Italian seasoning blend
- ½ teaspoon garlic powder

1. Preheat griddle to medium. Add oil and then zucchini rounds. Season with salt.
2. Cook 2 minutes and flip. Add a dollop of pizza sauce to each, sprinkle cheese over top, place a pepperoni slice on each, and season with Italian seasoning and garlic powder.
3. Lower griddle lid or cover with melting dome for 2 minutes until cheese is melted. Serve.

PER SERVING: Calories: 163 | Fat: 11g | Sodium: 501mg | Carbohydrates: 5g | Fiber: 1g | Sugar: 3g | Protein: 8g

BACON-WRAPPED PICKLE SPEARS

Pickle lovers are sure to be ecstatic about this fun snack. Mix it up by replacing the barbecue seasoning with any seasoning blend that you prefer.

PREP TIME MINUTES **10** ▲ COOK TIME MINUTES **9** ▲ SERVES **4**

- 8 refrigerated dill pickle spears
- 8 slices bacon
- 1 teaspoon barbecue seasoning blend
- ¼ cup ranch dressing

1. Pat pickle spears very dry with paper towels. Wrap a bacon slice around each pickle spear, overlapping it slightly and tucking in the end. Season all sides with barbecue seasoning blend.
2. Preheat griddle to medium-low. Place bacon-wrapped pickles on griddle.
3. Cook 7–9 minutes, turning with tongs several times, until bacon is crisped to your liking.
4. Let cool slightly before serving with ranch dressing for dipping.

PER SERVING: Calories: 119 | Fat: 8g | Sodium: 1,046mg | Carbohydrates: 2g | Fiber: 1g | Sugar: 1g | Protein: 8g

PRETZELS AND BEER CHEESE

This recipe calls for soft pretzel bites, but you could also use a 12-ounce package of regular frozen soft pretzels. If they are thawed, the cook time for the pretzels will be the same as those in this recipe.

PREP TIME MINUTES **5** ▲ COOK TIME MINUTES **12** ▲ SERVES **6**

- 4 ounces cream cheese
- 1 cup shredded Cheddar cheese
- ½ cup light beer
- 2 tablespoons Worcestershire sauce
- ½ teaspoon ground mustard
- 1 (12-ounce) package soft pretzel bites

1. Preheat griddle to medium-low. Place a small saucepan on griddle and add cream cheese to saucepan. Cook 4 minutes, stirring a few times to melt the cheese, then add Cheddar, beer, Worcestershire, and ground mustard. Cook 4 more minutes, stirring until melted and combined.
2. Add pretzel bites to griddle. Cook 4 minutes, flipping a few times, until warmed through. When cooking the pretzels, leave saucepan with beer cheese on griddle to keep warm, but if it starts bubbling, remove from griddle.
3. Serve pretzel bites with beer cheese for dipping.

PER SERVING: Calories: 295 | Fat: 11g | Sodium: 366mg | Carbohydrates: 34g | Fiber: 1g | Sugar: 2g | Protein: 10g

CHEESY MASHED POTATO CAKES

These cakes are a perfect way to enjoy mashed potatoes while camping! They are perfect on their own, or you can top them with sour cream and chives.

PREP TIME MINUTES **10** ▲ COOK TIME MINUTES **7** ▲ SERVES **6**

3 cups store-bought mashed potatoes

2 large eggs

1 cup shredded Cheddar cheese

⅓ cup all-purpose flour

½ teaspoon garlic powder

½ teaspoon kosher salt

2 tablespoons unsalted butter

1. In a medium bowl, place mashed potatoes, eggs, cheese, flour, garlic powder, and salt. Mix until combined.
2. Preheat griddle to medium. Add butter and, once melted, evenly spoon potato mixture onto griddle, making 12 cakes. Cook 3 minutes per side until golden brown. Serve warm.

PER SERVING: Calories: 278 | Fat: 15g | Sodium: 638mg | Carbohydrates: 24g | Fiber: 2g | Sugar: 2g | Protein: 9g

SANDWICHES AND WRAPS

There's a reason sandwiches and wraps are popular choices for camping meals . . . they are so quick and easy to make with minimal prep work. In this chapter, you'll find some unique recipes as well as some classic handheld options for lunch or a light dinner, including Chicken Bacon Ranch Subs, Burger and French Fry Wraps, Chili Dog Grilled Cheese, Vegetable Gyros, Pizza Pita Pockets, and Stuffed Sausage Sandwiches. Don't let the active pace of your camping adventures tempt you into skipping lunch or eating something processed from a package for convenience when you can cook some tasty, warm, and delicious meals in no time on your Blackstone!

CHILI DOG GRILLED CHEESE

This recipe takes two classics—the grilled cheese and the chili dog—and combines them into one delicious meal. It also makes holding and eating a drippy chili dog at a campsite way less messy.

PREP TIME MINUTES **10** ▲ COOK TIME MINUTES **9** ▲ SERVES **4**

4 beef hot dogs, cut in half lengthwise

2 tablespoons unsalted butter

8 slices white sandwich bread

8 (1-ounce) slices American cheese

1 cup canned chili

2 tablespoons yellow mustard

1. Preheat griddle to medium. Add hot dogs, cut side down, to griddle for 1 minute. Flip and cook 1 more minute. Use a burger press to keep them flat if desired. Lower heat to medium-low and move hot dogs to edge of griddle.
2. Add butter and, once melted, place 4 slices of bread on griddle. To each one, add a slice of cheese, 2 halves of a hot dog, ¼ cup chili, ½ tablespoon mustard, and a second slice of cheese. Then top each one with another slice of bread to make 4 sandwiches. Press down slightly with spatulas.
3. Cook 2–3 minutes per side until cheese is melted. If chili spills on the griddle, scoop it up with spatulas and place it on your plate
4. Let cool slightly, slice sandwiches in half, and serve.

PER SERVING: Calories: 562 | Fat: 30g | Sodium: 1,875mg | Carbohydrates: 46g | Fiber: 4g | Sugar: 10g | Protein: 24g

A can of chili is typically 15 or 16 ounces, and hot dogs usually come in packs of eight. So, you can plan to have this meal twice during your camping trip if you pack enough bread and cheese. That's two incredible meals with only a few ingredients!

CHICKEN BACON RANCH SUBS

This tasty sub sandwich features a classic trio of chicken, bacon, and ranch dressing. A garlic and herb, ranch, or Italian seasoning blend would be a nice addition to the chicken as well.

PREP TIME MINUTES **10** ▲ COOK TIME MINUTES **16** ▲ SERVES **4**

- 8 slices bacon
- 4 (4-ounce) thin-cut, boneless, skinless chicken breasts
- ½ teaspoon kosher salt
- ¼ teaspoon ground black pepper
- 4 (1-ounce) slices Swiss cheese
- 4 sub buns
- ½ cup ranch dressing

1. Preheat griddle to medium-low. Add bacon and cook 5–7 minutes, flipping a few times, until bacon is cooked to your liking. Remove bacon and set aside, but leave grease on griddle.
2. Place chicken on griddle and season with salt and pepper. Cook 4 minutes per side.
3. Put 2 slices cooked bacon onto each chicken breast and top with Swiss. Lower griddle lid or cover with melting dome 1 minute to melt cheese.
4. Place chicken on bottom sub buns, drizzle with ranch dressing, add top buns, and serve.

PER SERVING: Calories: 529 | Fat: 24g | Sodium: 946mg | Carbohydrates: 37g | Fiber: 2g | Sugar: 3g | Protein: 43g

BBQ ONION RING BURGERS

Using premade burger patties while camping is a huge time-saver. Add your favorite burger, barbecue, or steak seasoning blend if you'd like. Serve any extra onion rings as a side dish for a complete meal.

PREP TIME MINUTES **5** ▲ COOK TIME MINUTES **20** ▲ SERVES **4**

- 1 (16-ounce) bag frozen onion rings, thawed
- 4 (4-ounce) 80/20 beef burger patties
- ½ teaspoon kosher salt
- ¼ teaspoon ground black pepper
- 4 (1-ounce) slices American cheese
- 4 brioche burger buns
- ½ cup barbecue sauce

1. Preheat griddle to medium. Add onion rings in a single layer and cook 8–10 minutes, flipping with tongs a few times. Once crisp and golden brown, scoot onion rings to edge of griddle to keep warm.
2. Place burger patties on griddle and season with salt and pepper. Cook 3–4 minutes per side, depending on how you like your burgers cooked.
3. Place a slice of cheese on each burger. Lower griddle lid or cover with melting dome for 1 minute until cheese is melted. Place buns, cut side down, on griddle for 30 seconds to toast them.
4. Place each burger on a bottom bun, add a few onion rings, drizzle with barbecue sauce, and add top bun. Serve.

PER SERVING: Calories: 768 | Fat: 29g | Sodium: 1,730mg | Carbohydrates: 88g | Fiber: 4g | Sugar: 27g | Protein: 31g

PESTO AND TOMATO MELTS

This is a meatless sandwich with fresh ingredients that gets toasty and melty on the Blackstone. Mix it up with a multigrain or sourdough bread or by using a different kind of cheese.

PREP TIME MINUTES **5** ▲ COOK TIME MINUTES **7** ▲ SERVES **4**

- **2 tablespoons unsalted butter**
- **8 slices brioche sandwich bread**
- **8 (1-ounce) slices provolone cheese**
- **4 tablespoons pesto**
- **2 medium Roma tomatoes, ends removed and cut into 8 slices**

1. Preheat griddle to medium-low. Add butter and, once melted, lay 4 slices of bread on griddle.
2. On each slice of bread, place a slice of cheese, 1 tablespoon pesto, 2 tomato slices, a second slice of cheese, and top slice of bread. Use a spatula to press down slightly.
3. Cook 2–3 minutes per side until golden brown and cheese is melted. Slice sandwiches in half and serve.

PER SERVING: Calories: 525 | Fat: 27g | Sodium: 1,028mg | Carbohydrates: 46g | Fiber: 1g | Sugar: 7g | Protein: 22g

BURGER AND FRENCH FRY WRAPS

Why have a burger with a side of fries when you can have the whole meal wrapped into an individual handheld package? No plates required for this one—it's the perfect campsite meal!

PREP TIME MINUTES **10** ▲ COOK TIME MINUTES **12** ▲ SERVES **4**

- 4 ounces frozen French fries, thawed
- 4 (4-ounce) 80/20 beef burger patties
- ½ teaspoon kosher salt
- ¼ teaspoon ground black pepper
- 4 (10-inch) soft flour tortillas
- 4 (1-ounce) slices American cheese
- 4 tablespoons ketchup
- 1 tablespoon vegetable oil

1. Preheat griddle to medium. Put fries on one side of griddle and burgers on other side. Season both with salt and pepper. Cook both 6–8 minutes until fries are crisped and golden brown and burgers are cooked to your liking, flipping burgers halfway through. Remove fries and burgers, scrape griddle clean, and lower heat to medium-low.
2. Lay tortillas flat on your work surface. Place a burger, 1 slice of cheese, 1 tablespoon ketchup, and a few fries in the center of each tortilla. Fold edges of each tortilla in, overlapping slightly, completely sealing each into the shape of a hexagon.
3. Add oil to griddle and place wraps seam side down. Cook 2 minutes, then flip and cook on the other side 2 more minutes, until golden brown. Serve immediately.

PER SERVING: Calories: 537 | Fat: 20g | Sodium: 1,449mg | Carbohydrates: 51g | Fiber: 3g | Sugar: 8g | Protein: 27g

BURGER WRAP VARIATIONS

Feel free to add pickles, lettuce, or any other burger toppings to your wraps as long as you have room to pack them. You could also swap out the ketchup for tartar sauce or burger sauce. Another option is using onion rings in place of the fries and adding barbecue sauce.

ITALIAN SAUSAGE AND PEPPER SLIDERS

This meal is always a hit at the campsite, but it does require extra napkins. You should preslice the slider buns and dice the peppers and onions at home to avoid extra work at the campground.

PREP TIME MINUTES **15** ▲ COOK TIME MINUTES **10** ▲ SERVES **4**

- **1 tablespoon olive oil**
- **1 medium red bell pepper, seeded and diced**
- **1 medium yellow onion, peeled and diced**
- **½ teaspoon kosher salt**
- **¼ teaspoon ground black pepper**
- **1 pound sweet Italian ground sausage**
- **1 (12-count) package slider buns, not separated, sliced horizontally to separate tops from bottoms**
- **1 cup marinara sauce**
- **6 (1-ounce) slices provolone cheese**

1. Preheat griddle to medium. Add oil, bell pepper, onion, salt, and pepper. Cook 3 minutes, mixing a few times with spatulas.
2. Add sausage to griddle with pepper-onion mixture. Cook 6 more minutes, mixing and breaking sausage apart with spatulas. Scoot this mixture to edge of griddle.
3. Place section of bottom buns on griddle, cut side up. Use spatulas to transfer sausage mixture to bottom buns. Spoon marinara sauce over top and add cheese, overlapping slices slightly, then add top slider buns.
4. Lower griddle lid or cover with melting dome 1 minute until cheese is melted. Slice sliders and serve.

PER SERVING: Calories: 851 | Fat: 46g | Sodium: 2,339mg | Carbohydrates: 66g | Fiber: 5g | Sugar: 14g | Protein: 42g

FRENCH DIP SUBS

This is such a quick and easy meal to prepare on the Blackstone. You can also try adding horseradish sauce for a little extra zing.

PREP TIME MINUTES **5** ▲ COOK TIME MINUTES **5** ▲ SERVES **4**

1 (1-ounce) packet au jus sauce mix

1 pound sliced deli roast beef

8 (1-ounce) slices provolone cheese

4 sub buns, sliced

1. Preheat griddle to high. Place a small saucepan on griddle and add au jus packet and 3 cups water. Bring to a boil and cook 1 minute, stirring a few times. Lower heat to medium and move saucepan to edge of griddle.
2. Dip each slice of roast beef into au jus for a second and then place beef on griddle in 4 piles, making sure each pile has several slices and is a similar shape to sub buns. Cook 2 minutes, flip, and cook 1 more minute.
3. Place 2 slices of cheese over each pile of beef. Close griddle lid or cover with melting dome 1 minute until cheese is melted. Transfer each pile to a sub bun and serve with remaining au jus for dipping.

PER SERVING: Calories: 561 | Fat: 24g | Sodium: 2,534mg | Carbohydrates: 40g | Fiber: 2g | Sugar: 4g | Protein: 44g

BUFFALO RANCH CHICKEN BURGERS

This recipe is a celebration of both chicken wings and burgers. It is helpful to wear rubber gloves when forming the patties for easier cleanup. Blue cheese crumbles are an optional topping for these fun burgers.

PREP TIME MINUTES **10** ▲ COOK TIME MINUTES **9** ▲ SERVES **4**

1 pound ground chicken

1 tablespoon dry ranch seasoning

½ cup buffalo wing sauce, divided

1 tablespoon vegetable oil

4 hamburger buns

½ cup shredded lettuce

1. Put chicken in a medium bowl with ranch seasoning and ¼ cup buffalo sauce. Combine with your hands and form mixture into 4 patties.
2. Preheat griddle to medium. Add oil and place chicken patties on griddle. Cook 4 minutes per side.
3. Place buns, cut side down, on griddle for 30 seconds to toast. Add a patty to each bottom bun, drizzle with remaining ¼ cup buffalo sauce, add lettuce, then add top burger bun. Serve.

PER SERVING: Calories: 327 | Fat: 14g | Sodium: 1,401mg | Carbohydrates: 23g | Fiber: 1g | Sugar: 3g | Protein: 25g

SHRIMP PO'BOYS

Here is an easy way to enjoy this amazing sandwich in the great outdoors. You could also toss the shrimp in buffalo sauce after cooking or drizzle it with ranch dressing for another variation.

PREP TIME MINUTES **5** ▲ COOK TIME MINUTES **7** ▲ SERVES **4**

1 tablespoon vegetable oil

1 (12-ounce) box frozen breaded popcorn shrimp, thawed

1 teaspoon seafood seasoning blend

4 sub buns, sliced

½ cup remoulade sauce

1½ cups shredded lettuce

1. Preheat griddle to medium. Add oil and then shrimp. Cook 5–6 minutes or until shrimp is crisped and golden brown. Sprinkle seafood seasoning over top and toss to coat.
2. Place sub buns, cut side down, on griddle for 30 seconds to toast them.
3. Spread remoulade sauce on bottoms and tops of buns. To bottom buns, add shrimp and then lettuce. Place on top buns, pressing down slightly. Serve.

PER SERVING: Calories: 614 | Fat: 34g | Sodium: 1,152mg | Carbohydrates: 62g | Fiber: 3g | Sugar: 8g | Protein: 18g

REUBEN DOGS

This is a twist on the classic Reuben sandwich. It has the same flavors but uses hot dogs in place of the traditional corned beef.

PREP TIME MINUTES **5** ▲ COOK TIME MINUTES **6** ▲ SERVES **4**

8 beef hot dogs

8 hot dog buns

8 (1-ounce) slices Swiss cheese

½ cup Russian dressing

1 cup sauerkraut

1. Use a sharp knife to make several crisscross cuts into the hot dogs on both sides, about a centimeter deep. This will help create crispy edges all over the hot dogs.
2. Preheat griddle to medium. Add hot dogs and cook 5 minutes, turning a few times. Move hot dogs to edge of griddle.
3. Place buns on griddle, opened slightly with cut side down, for 30 seconds. Turn them over and place 1 slice of Swiss in the center of each, folding cheese if needed. Cover with melting dome 30 seconds until cheese melts slightly.
4. Place hot dogs into the buns and add Russian dressing and sauerkraut to each. Serve.

PER SERVING: Calories: 757 | Fat: 44g | Sodium: 1,637mg | Carbohydrates: 50g | Fiber: 3g | Sugar: 9g | Protein: 34g

For a fun camping tradition, try a friendly hot dog topping contest with your family or other families at the campground. Everyone comes up with their own hot dog creation, and everyone votes on their favorite!

CAJUN CATFISH SANDWICHES

If fishing is part of your camping experience, you may be lucky enough to have fresh-caught catfish for this meal. Tilapia, haddock, whitefish, or flounder are all great substitutions.

PREP TIME MINUTES **10** ▲ COOK TIME MINUTES **11** ▲ SERVES **4**

- 4 (6-ounce) catfish fillets
- 1 teaspoon Cajun seasoning blend
- 2 tablespoons olive oil
- 4 hamburger buns
- 1 cup shredded lettuce
- ¼ cup tartar sauce

1. Pat fish dry with paper towels and season both sides of each fillet with Cajun seasoning.
2. Preheat griddle to medium-low. Add oil and then catfish. Cook 8–10 minutes total, flipping halfway through the cooking time until fish is cooked through.
3. Place buns, cut side down, on griddle for 30 seconds to toast them.
4. Place 1 catfish fillet on each bottom bun and top with ¼ cup lettuce, 1 tablespoon tartar sauce, and top bun. Serve.

PER SERVING: Calories: 382 | Fat: 17g | Sodium: 444mg | Carbohydrates: 22g | Fiber: 1g | Sugar: 3g | Protein: 30g

VEGETABLE GYROS

Here is a meatless version of the traditional gyro that is just as hearty, filling, and flavorful. Slicing the vegetables at home and storing them in plastic bags saves time and hassle at the campground.

PREP TIME MINUTES **15** ▲ COOK TIME MINUTES **10** ▲ SERVES **4**

- 1 tablespoon olive oil
- 1 medium red onion, peeled and sliced
- 1 medium red bell pepper, seeded and sliced
- 8 ounces white mushrooms, sliced
- 1 tablespoon dried oregano
- ½ teaspoon kosher salt
- ¼ teaspoon ground black pepper
- 4 (4-ounce) naan flatbreads
- 1 cup tzatziki sauce

1. Preheat griddle to medium. Add oil, onion, bell pepper, mushrooms, oregano, salt, and pepper. Cook 9 minutes, mixing with spatulas.
2. Scoot vegetables to edge of griddle. Place flatbreads on griddle 30 seconds per side to warm them.
3. Place vegetables in the center of each flatbread, spoon tzatziki over top, fold, and serve.

PER SERVING: Calories: 514 | Fat: 15g | Sodium: 1,424mg | Carbohydrates: 75g | Fiber: 4g | Sugar: 14g | Protein: 18g

BEEF AND BEAN BURRITOS

This dish is very similar to tacos but is more camping-friendly and easier to eat. Plates are not even required with this meal.

PREP TIME MINUTES **5** ▲ COOK TIME MINUTES **12** ▲ SERVES **5**

- 1 pound 80/20 ground beef
- 1 (1-ounce) packet taco seasoning blend
- 10 (8-inch) soft flour tortillas
- 1 (16-ounce) can refried beans
- 2 cups shredded Cheddar cheese
- 2 tablespoons vegetable oil

1. Preheat griddle to medium. Add beef and cook 5 minutes, breaking meat apart with spatulas. Add taco seasoning and ¼ cup water. Cook 2 more minutes, mixing. Remove beef, scrape griddle, and lower heat to medium-low.
2. Place tortillas on griddle 30 seconds to warm them. Remove tortillas and place them on your work surface. Spread beans in center of each tortilla, then add taco meat and cheese. Fold sides in and roll burritos tightly.
3. Add oil to griddle and place burritos seam-side down. Cook 1–2 minutes per side until crisped and golden brown. Serve warm.

PER SERVING: Calories: 792 | Fat: 35g | Sodium: 1,787mg | Carbohydrates: 66g | Fiber: 7g | Sugar: 5g | Protein: 41g

PIZZA PITA POCKETS

You can add any of your favorite pizza toppings to these pita pockets. The best part is when some of the cheese melts out onto the griddle, creating crispy, cheesy goodness.

PREP TIME MINUTES **5** ▲ COOK TIME MINUTES **9** ▲ SERVES **4**

4 pieces pita bread

½ cup pizza sauce

32 slices pepperoni

2 cups shredded mozzarella cheese

3 tablespoons unsalted butter

½ teaspoon Italian seasoning blend

½ teaspoon garlic powder

1. Slice pita breads in half, forming two semicircle pockets. Spread some pizza sauce in each pocket, add pepperoni slices, and stuff cheese in each pocket.
2. Preheat griddle to medium-low. Add butter and, once melted, place stuffed pitas on the griddle.
3. Cook 8 minutes total, flipping a few times. Use spatulas to scoot melted cheese back into the pockets as needed. Sprinkle Italian seasoning and garlic powder on both sides of pita bread during the last minute.
4. Remove once cheese is melted and pita bread is slightly crisp and golden brown. Let cool slightly before serving.

PER SERVING: Calories: 469 | Fat: 22g | Sodium: 1,007mg | Carbohydrates: 40g | Fiber: 2g | Sugar: 3g | Protein: 20g

STUFFED SAUSAGE SANDWICHES

Cheesy loaded sausages just taste better when served on buns and eaten outside in nature. Mix up this recipe by using different sausages, toppings, and cheeses if you'd like.

PREP TIME MINUTES **5** ▲ COOK TIME MINUTES **10** ▲ SERVES **4**

4 (4-ounce) Italian sausage links

½ cup marinara sauce

1 cup shredded mozzarella cheese

½ cup sliced pickled banana pepper rings

4 hot dog buns

1. Make a long slice down the center, lengthwise, in each sausage link. Cut about 1 inch deep and then flatten each link, opening the slice slightly to create a pocket.
2. Preheat griddle to medium. Place sausage links on griddle, cut side down, and cook 4 minutes. Flip and cook 4 more minutes.
3. Spoon marinara sauce into the opened part of each sausage, sprinkle cheese over each, and add banana peppers over top. Lower griddle lid or cover with melting dome 2 minutes until cheese is melted.
4. Serve stuffed sausages in buns.

PER SERVING: Calories: 516 | Fat: 30g | Sodium: 1,711mg | Carbohydrates: 29g | Fiber: 1g | Sugar: 5g | Protein: 27g

You could add ricotta cheese and leave out the banana peppers for a lasagna-stuffed sandwich version. Or use chicken sausage links, with buffalo sauce, Cheddar, and blue cheese crumbles. A Reuben version with turkey sausage links, sauerkraut, Swiss cheese, and Russian dressing is another favorite variety of Stuffed Sausage Sandwiches.

CAMP MAIN DISHES

In this chapter, you will find some complete dinner recipes ranging from extra simple to extraordinary, such as Stir-Fried Vegetable Ramen; Cheesy Taco Tortellini; Hawaiian Fried Rice; Turkey, Green Beans, and Cranberries; Lemon Shrimp and Asparagus; Hot Honey Pork and Apples; Unstuffed Bell Peppers; and Hibachi Steak Kebabs. And because you make these dishes on your Blackstone griddle, they come together in no time at all, so all those hungry campers won't have a hangry meltdown when dinnertime rolls around. Plus, many of these recipes include options to swap out ingredients and seasonings so you can adapt the recipes to fit your group's taste preferences. With so many dinner ideas to choose from, one is sure to hit the spot with your campers!

ITALIAN CHICKEN, GREEN BEANS, AND TOMATOES

Nothing beats a hearty meal with fresh ingredients after a long day of fun in the outdoors. You can cut the chicken at home and even marinate it at home for convenience at the campsite.

PREP TIME MINUTES **70*** ▲ COOK TIME MINUTES **12** ▲ SERVES **4**

- **1 pound boneless, skinless chicken thighs, cut into bite-sized pieces**
- **¾ cup Italian dressing**
- **2 tablespoons olive oil**
- **1 pound green beans, trimmed**
- **1 pint whole grape tomatoes**
- **1 tablespoon Italian seasoning blend**
- **1 teaspoon garlic powder**
- **½ teaspoon kosher salt**
- **¼ teaspoon ground black pepper**

* INCLUDES MARINATING TIME

1. Put chicken in a gallon-sized plastic bag and add Italian dressing. Massage bag until combined and marinate 1 hour or up to overnight.
2. Preheat griddle to medium. Add oil and then green beans. Lower griddle lid or cover with melting dome 4 minutes, mixing with spatulas halfway through the cooking time.
3. Add chicken with marinade, tomatoes, Italian seasoning, garlic powder, salt, and pepper. Cook 8 minutes, mixing everything together with spatulas a few times. Serve warm.

PER SERVING: Calories: 279 | Fat: 11g | Sodium: 730mg | Carbohydrates: 17g | Fiber: 4g | Sugar: 10g | Protein: 28g

ITALIAN SUB SALADS

This salad is very filling and a nice, light dinner option, especially on a hot day. Add tomatoes, banana peppers, and sliced onions if desired.

PREP TIME MINUTES **10** ▲ COOK TIME MINUTES **5** ▲ SERVES **4**

- 2 tablespoons olive oil
- ½ pound diced deli ham
- ½ pound diced deli salami
- 3 cups diced Italian bread
- 1 (24-ounce) bag garden salad mix
- 1 cup shredded mozzarella cheese
- 6 ounces Italian dressing

1. Preheat griddle to medium-low. Add oil, ham, salami, and bread. Cook 5 minutes, mixing with spatulas a few times.
2. Remove once bread is slightly toasted and let cool slightly.
3. Put salad mix in a large bowl with ham, salami, bread, cheese, and dressing. Toss until evenly mixed and serve.

PER SERVING: Calories: 593 | Fat: 38g | Sodium: 2,301mg | Carbohydrates: 30g | Fiber: 3g | Sugar: 10g | Protein: 33g

In place of the Italian bread, try adding tortellini to your salad. Add a 10-ounce bag of frozen cheese tortellini that has been thawed to your Blackstone over medium heat. Add ¼ cup water and lower griddle lid or cover with melting dome for 5 minutes. Remove the dome or lid to add ¼ cup more water and toss with spatulas halfway through. Let cool and then toss into your salad.

STIR-FRIED VEGETABLE RAMEN

This is a vegetarian meal, but if you want to add some meat, you can add chicken or steak. A fried egg over the top is also a nice addition.

PREP TIME MINUTES **10** ▲ COOK TIME MINUTES **10** ▲ SERVES **6**

- **2 tablespoons vegetable oil**
- **8 ounces sliced white button mushrooms**
- **8 ounces sugar snap peas**
- **1 medium red bell pepper, seeded and sliced**
- **½ teaspoon kosher salt**
- **¼ teaspoon ground black pepper**
- **3 (3-ounce) packages ramen noodles, minus seasoning packets**
- **½ cup Bachan's Japanese Barbecue sauce**

1. Preheat griddle to medium. Add oil, mushrooms, snap peas, bell pepper, salt, and pepper to one side of the griddle. To the other side, add noodles and ¼ cup water, then cover noodles with melting dome.
2. Cook vegetables and noodles 4 minutes, mixing vegetables with spatulas a few times. Mix noodles halfway through cooking time and add ¼ cup more water if needed.
3. Use spatulas to bring everything together on the griddle. Add Japanese barbecue sauce and cook 6 more minutes. Serve warm.

PER SERVING: Calories: 305 | Fat: 12g | Sodium: 1,108mg | Carbohydrates: 43g | Fiber: 3g | Sugar: 14g | Protein: 7g

CHEESY TACO TORTELLINI

Taco ingredients combined with pasta in a luscious, creamy cheese sauce is a camping meal that no one will be able to resist.

PREP TIME MINUTES **5** ▲ COOK TIME MINUTES **10** ▲ SERVES **6**

- 1 (20-ounce) bag frozen cheese tortellini, thawed
- 1 pound 80/20 ground beef
- 1 (1-ounce) packet taco seasoning blend
- 1 (10-ounce) can Rotel tomatoes
- 1½ cups heavy cream
- ½ teaspoon kosher salt
- ¼ teaspoon ground black pepper
- 1½ cups shredded Monterey jack cheese

1. Preheat griddle to medium. Add tortellini and ¼ cup water to one side of griddle and cover with melting dome. Add ground beef to the other side of griddle.
2. Cook tortellini and beef 4 minutes, breaking beef apart with spatulas. Mix tortellini halfway through the cooking time with spatulas and add ¼ cup more water before covering again.
3. Add ½ cup water and taco seasoning to beef. Cook 2 minutes, mixing together with tortellini.
4. Add Rotel, cream, salt, and pepper. Cook 3 minutes, mixing and keeping cream contained with spatulas until it thickens.
5. Add cheese and mix everything together. Cook 1 more minute until cheese melts and then serve warm.

PER SERVING: Calories: 675 | Fat: 40g | Sodium: 1,175mg | Carbohydrates: 40g | Fiber: 7g | Sugar: 4g | Protein: 32g

Make dinners while camping that will leave you with delicious leftovers for tomorrow's lunch or dinner. Buy extra ingredients if you have to. Having a meal almost completely prepared at the end of a busy day or for a quick and easy lunch is the key to a happy camping trip for everyone, especially the cook.

BBQ SALMON AND BROCCOLI

This healthy meal has only a few ingredients but is full of flavor! You can also substitute a pound of sliced zucchini, halved Brussels sprouts, or chopped asparagus in place of the broccoli and still follow the same cook time and directions.

PREP TIME MINUTES **5** ▲ COOK TIME MINUTES **8** ▲ SERVES **4**

- 2 tablespoons olive oil
- 4 (5-ounce) salmon fillets
- 1 pound broccoli florets
- 1½ tablespoons barbecue seasoning blend
- ½ teaspoon kosher salt
- ¼ teaspoon ground black pepper
- ½ cup barbecue sauce

1. Preheat griddle to medium. Add oil and then place salmon fillets skin-side down on one side of griddle. Place broccoli on other side.
2. Sprinkle salmon and broccoli with barbecue seasoning, salt, and pepper. Cook 8 minutes, using spatulas to flip salmon halfway through cooking time and toss broccoli a few times.
3. Serve with barbecue sauce for dipping.

PER SERVING: Calories: 454 | Fat: 22g | Sodium: 1,110mg | Carbohydrates: 22g | Fiber: 3g | Sugar: 14g | Protein: 32g

PORK AND GRAPE KEBABS AND RICE

This is a Spanish-inspired recipe for a unique camping dinner experience. The pop of sweetness from the grapes with the savory pork is a heavenly combo.

PREP TIME MINUTES **10** ▲ COOK TIME MINUTES **6** ▲ SERVES **4**

1 pound pork chops, cut into bite-sized pieces

2 tablespoons olive oil, divided

2 teaspoons smoked paprika

½ teaspoon garlic powder

½ teaspoon kosher salt

¼ teaspoon ground black pepper

1 pound seedless red grapes

1 (17.3-ounce) pouch Ben's Spanish Style Ready Rice

1. Place pork in a medium bowl. Add 1 tablespoon oil, paprika, garlic powder, salt, and pepper. Toss until combined.
2. On four kebab skewers, alternate pork and grapes.
3. Preheat griddle to medium. Add remaining 1 tablespoon oil and then place kebabs on one side of griddle. Put rice on the other side of griddle, add ¼ cup water, and cover rice with melting dome.
4. Cook kebabs and rice 6 minutes, turning kebabs a few times during cooking time and mixing rice with spatulas. Add ¼ cup more water to rice if needed before covering again. Serve kebabs over rice.

PER SERVING: Calories: 523 | Fat: 13g | Sodium: 552mg | Carbohydrates: 66g | Fiber: 2g | Sugar: 19g | Protein: 32g

GARLIC BUTTER STEAK BITES AND POTATOES

Oh, that classic steak and potatoes combo hits the spot every time! Precut the steak and garlic at home and pack them in plastic bags so everything is all ready to go on the Blackstone.

PREP TIME MINUTES **10** ▲ COOK TIME MINUTES **16** ▲ SERVES **4**

- **5 tablespoons unsalted butter, divided**
- **1 (20-ounce) bag diced Simply Potatoes**
- **1 pound sirloin steak, cut into bite-sized pieces**
- **1 tablespoon steak seasoning blend**
- **½ teaspoon kosher salt**
- **¼ teaspoon ground black pepper**
- **8 cloves garlic, peeled and minced**

1. Preheat griddle to medium. Add 1 tablespoon butter and, once melted, add potatoes and ¼ cup water. Lower griddle lid or cover with melting dome. Cook potatoes 8 minutes, adding ¼ cup more water and mixing halfway through the cooking time. Raise lid or set dome aside.
2. Add steak, steak seasoning, salt, and pepper to griddle. Mix everything together with spatulas and cook 5 more minutes.
3. Add remaining 4 tablespoons butter and garlic and cook 2 more minutes, mixing as butter melts. Serve warm.

PER SERVING: Calories: 467 | Fat: 24g | Sodium: 889mg | Carbohydrates: 28g | Fiber: 3g | Sugar: 0g | Protein: 27g

HAWAIIAN FRIED RICE

Spam is very shelf-stable, which makes it a perfect camping ingredient, but if you don't like it, feel free to use diced deli ham instead. The Japanese barbecue sauce in this recipe is a sweet soy-based sauce that is perfect for fried rice.

PREP TIME MINUTES **5** ▲ COOK TIME MINUTES **11** ▲ SERVES **4**

- 3 tablespoons unsalted butter, divided
- 1 (17.3-ounce) pouch Ben's Jasmine Ready Rice
- 1 (12-ounce) container Spam, diced
- 2 large eggs
- 1 (8-ounce) can pineapple chunks, drained
- ⅓ cup Bachan's Japanese Barbecue sauce

1. Preheat griddle to medium. Add 1 tablespoon butter and, once melted, add rice with ¼ cup water. Lower griddle lid or cover with melting dome for 2 minutes.
2. Add Spam to empty space on griddle, mixing with spatulas for 2 minutes. Break rice apart with spatulas while Spam cooks.
3. Crack eggs over rice. Add pineapple to Spam. Cook rice and Spam 2 more minutes, mixing both while keeping separate.
4. Mix everything together with spatulas. Add remaining 2 tablespoons butter and drizzle barbecue sauce over top. Cook and mix 4 more minutes. Serve warm.

PER SERVING: Calories: 664 | Fat: 35g | Sodium: 1,907mg | Carbohydrates: 66g | Fiber: 1g | Sugar: 19g | Protein: 20g

The Japanese barbecue sauce is just one option for this fried rice. You could use the same amount of soy sauce instead or even a teriyaki or stir-fry sauce. Adding a cup of frozen diced peas and carrots is also a nice touch. Other meat options include diced chicken or steak—just add 3 minutes to the cook time to make sure the meat is cooked through.

SALMON CAESAR SALAD

A healthy campsite dinner on the Blackstone doesn't get any easier than this recipe. Swap out the type of salad kit and try some different toppings and dressings to add variety to this meal.

PREP TIME MINUTES **10** ▲ COOK TIME MINUTES **8** ▲ SERVES **4**

- 1 tablespoon olive oil
- 4 (4-ounce) salmon fillets
- 1 tablespoon garlic herb seasoning
- 2 (10-ounce) Caesar salad kits

1. Preheat griddle to medium. Add oil and then salmon fillets, skin side down. Season salmon with garlic herb seasoning.
2. Cook salmon 8 minutes total, flipping with tongs halfway through the cooking time. Remove and let cool slightly.
3. In a large bowl, assemble salad kits according to package directions.
4. Divide salad between four bowls or plates and top each with a salmon fillet to serve.

PER SERVING: Calories: 486 | Fat: 34g | Sodium: 592mg | Carbohydrates: 10g | Fiber: 3g | Sugar: 3g | Protein: 29g

TERIYAKI TURKEY AND ZUCCHINI RICE BOWLS

These super simple rice bowls can be jazzed up in a variety of ways, including adding sriracha or a drizzle of yum yum sauce over the top, or garnishing with sesame seeds, cilantro, or scallions.

PREP TIME MINUTES **10** ▲ COOK TIME MINUTES **10** ▲ SERVES **4**

2 tablespoons vegetable oil, divided

1 (17.3-ounce) pouch Ben's Jasmine Ready Rice

1½ pounds turkey breast tenderloins, cut into bite-sized pieces

1 medium zucchini, diced into bite-sized pieces

½ teaspoon kosher salt

¼ teaspoon ground black pepper

½ cup teriyaki sauce

1. Preheat griddle to medium. Add 1 tablespoon oil to griddle. On one side of griddle, add rice and ¼ cup water. Lower griddle lid or cover with melting dome for 2 minutes.
2. To the empty side of griddle, add remaining 1 tablespoon oil, turkey, zucchini, salt, and pepper. Cook 6 minutes, mixing turkey and zucchini while also breaking apart and flipping the rice a few times.
3. Add teriyaki sauce to turkey and zucchini, mix, and cook 2 more minutes.
4. Place rice in four bowls and then top with teriyaki turkey and zucchini. Serve warm.

PER SERVING: Calories: 503 | Fat: 11g | Sodium: 1,771mg | Carbohydrates: 49g | Fiber: 1g | Sugar: 6g | Protein: 47g

TURKEY, GREEN BEANS, AND CRANBERRIES

This is the ultimate fall dinner, kind of like a mini version of Thanksgiving at the campground. This dish is so yummy served with Biscuits with Honey Butter or Cheesy Mashed Potato Cakes, both in Chapter 3.

PREP TIME MINUTES **10** ▲ COOK TIME MINUTES **13** ▲ SERVES **4**

4 tablespoons unsalted butter, divided

1 pound green beans, trimmed

1½ pounds turkey breast tenderloins, cut into bite-sized pieces

1 tablespoon dried sage

1 tablespoon dried thyme

½ teaspoon kosher salt

¼ teaspoon ground black pepper

¾ cup dried cranberries

1. Preheat griddle to medium. Add 1 tablespoon butter and, once melted, add green beans. Lower griddle lid or cover with melting dome 5 minutes, mixing with spatulas a few times.
2. Add turkey, sage, thyme, salt, and pepper. Cook 5 more minutes, mixing everything together with spatulas.
3. Add cranberries and remaining 3 tablespoons butter. Cook 2 more minutes and serve warm.

PER SERVING: Calories: 409 | Fat: 14g | Sodium: 383mg | Carbohydrates: 27g | Fiber: 5g | Sugar: 18g | Protein: 43g

CHICKEN AND BEAN CHILAQUILES

This recipe takes some simple shortcuts, like using store-bought tortilla chips and salsa, to make this traditional Mexican dish very camping-friendly. Prepare the chicken and beans at home and store them in plastic bags to make this meal even easier to prepare at the campsite!

PREP TIME MINUTES **10** ▲ COOK TIME MINUTES **11** ▲ SERVES **6**

- 1 tablespoon vegetable oil
- 1 pound boneless, skinless chicken thighs, cut into bite-sized pieces
- 1 tablespoon taco seasoning blend
- 6 cups tortilla chips
- 1 (14-ounce) can black beans, drained and rinsed
- 1 (16-ounce) jar salsa verde
- 1½ cups shredded Cheddar cheese
- ½ cup crumbled cotija cheese

1. Preheat griddle to medium. Add oil, chicken, and taco seasoning. Cook 7 minutes, mixing with spatulas.
2. Add chips, beans, and salsa. Gently combine with spatulas and cook 2 more minutes.
3. Sprinkle Cheddar over top and lower griddle lid or cover with melting dome 1–2 minutes until cheese is melted.
4. Remove from griddle and spoon onto plates. Serve with cotija sprinkled over top.

PER SERVING: Calories: 509 | Fat: 23g | Sodium: 1,269mg | Carbohydrates: 37g | Fiber: 6g | Sugar: 5g | Protein: 28g

Topping ideas for tacos, nachos, and chilaquiles are endless, but it's not always convenient to pack up all the extras for just one dinner. Plan ahead by organizing a few different meals that would be amazing with toppings such as sour cream, pickled red onions, lime wedges, jalapeños, and fresh cilantro. That way, you can justify the extra space when packing these ingredients.

ITALIAN VEGETABLE STIR-FRY

Here is a delicious meatless dish with bold flavors. Slice the vegetables at home and store them in a gallon-sized plastic bag for convenience at the campsite.

PREP TIME MINUTES **10** ▲ COOK TIME MINUTES **15** ▲ SERVES **4**

- **2 tablespoons olive oil, divided**
- **1 (20-ounce) bag diced Simply Potatoes**
- **8 ounces baby portobello mushrooms, sliced**
- **1 medium red bell pepper, seeded and sliced**
- **1 medium red onion, peeled and sliced**
- **1 tablespoon Italian seasoning blend**
- **½ teaspoon kosher salt**
- **¼ teaspoon ground black pepper**
- **½ cup Italian dressing**

1. Preheat griddle to medium. Add 1 tablespoon oil, potatoes, and ¼ cup water. Lower griddle lid or cover with melting dome. Cook potatoes 5 minutes, adding ¼ cup more water and mixing halfway through the cooking time. Raise lid or set dome aside.
2. Add remaining 1 tablespoon oil, mushrooms, bell pepper, onion, Italian seasoning, salt, and pepper. Mix everything with spatulas and cook 8–9 more minutes until vegetables are cooked to your liking.
3. Add Italian dressing and combine with spatulas 1 more minute before serving.

PER SERVING: Calories: 273 | Fat: 12g | Sodium: 623mg | Carbohydrates: 36g | Fiber: 4g | Sugar: 7g | Protein: 5g

BRATS, PEPPERS, AND PIEROGIES

This Polish-inspired meal is a creative way to enjoy brats in the great outdoors. Simplify this meal by packing already-sliced peppers and onions, and add any seasoning blend of your choice.

PREP TIME MINUTES **10** ▲ COOK TIME MINUTES **10** ▲ SERVES **4**

- 1 (16-ounce) package frozen potato and cheese pierogies, thawed
- 2 tablespoons olive oil
- 1 medium red bell pepper, seeded and sliced
- 1 medium green bell pepper, seeded and sliced
- 1 medium red onion, peeled and sliced
- ½ teaspoon kosher salt
- ¼ teaspoon ground black pepper
- 1 pound brats, sliced into 2-inch pieces
- 1 (16-ounce) jar Alfredo sauce

1. Preheat griddle to medium. Add pierogies to one side of griddle, squirt with 2 tablespoons water, and cover with melting dome. To the other side of griddle, add oil, bell peppers, onion, salt, and pepper.
2. Cook for 3 minutes, flipping pierogies with tongs halfway through the cooking time and adding 2 more tablespoons water before covering again. Mix vegetables a few times with spatulas.
3. Add brats and pierogies to vegetables and cook and mix with spatulas 5 minutes.
4. Add Alfredo sauce and combine with spatulas 2 more minutes. Serve warm.

PER SERVING: Calories: 838 | Fat: 61g | Sodium: 2,419mg | Carbohydrates: 44g | Fiber: 2g | Sugar: 4g | Protein: 25g

CABBAGE, BACON, AND POTATOES

This is a rustic cowboy-style meal that is meant to be enjoyed with friends and family around the campfire. You can also add your favorite seasoning blend of choice if desired.

PREP TIME MINUTES **10** ▲ COOK TIME MINUTES **22** ▲ SERVES **4**

8 slices bacon

1 (20-ounce) bag diced Simply Potatoes

1 medium head green cabbage, sliced thin

½ teaspoon kosher salt

¼ teaspoon ground black pepper

1 bunch scallions, sliced

2 tablespoons unsalted butter

1. Preheat griddle to medium-low. Lay bacon slices on griddle and cook 5–7 minutes, flipping a few times. Remove bacon, leaving bacon grease on griddle, and raise heat to medium.
2. Add potatoes to griddle along with ¼ cup water. Lower griddle lid or cover with melting dome. Cook potatoes 7 minutes, adding ¼ cup more water and mixing halfway through the cooking time. Raise lid or set dome aside.
3. Add cabbage, salt, and pepper to griddle. Cook 6 minutes, combining with potatoes.
4. Crumble bacon over top and add scallions and butter. Cook 2 more minutes, mixing. Serve warm.

PER SERVING: Calories: 327 | Fat: 13g | Sodium: 755mg | Carbohydrates: 40g | Fiber: 8g | Sugar: 7g | Protein: 13g

HOT HONEY PORK AND APPLES

Succulent pork chops griddled to perfection and topped with sweet and spicy apples is a match made in heaven! As another recipe option, you can replace the hot honey with the same amount of cinnamon-flavored whiskey.

PREP TIME MINUTES **5** ▲ COOK TIME MINUTES **8** ▲ SERVES **4**

- 4 (6-ounce, 1-inch-thick) bone-in pork chops
- ½ teaspoon kosher salt
- ¼ teaspoon ground black pepper
- 2 medium Honeycrisp apples, unpeeled, cored, and diced
- 1 tablespoon olive oil
- 4 tablespoons unsalted butter
- ¼ cup hot honey

1. Season pork with salt and pepper on both sides.
2. Preheat griddle to medium. Put apples on one side of griddle and add oil and pork to the other side.
3. Cook apples and pork 8 minutes total, flipping pork a few times and mixing apples with spatulas. Add butter and hot honey to apples during last 2 minutes of cooking, mixing together.
4. Serve pork topped with the hot honey apples.

PER SERVING: Calories: 577 | Fat: 33g | Sodium: 346mg | Carbohydrates: 29g | Fiber: 2g | Sugar: 26g | Protein: 33g

LEMON SHRIMP AND ASPARAGUS

This is a light griddle meal with bright flavors. Add a fresh herb such as basil, thyme, or chives to the shrimp during the last minute to bump up the flavor even more.

PREP TIME MINUTES **5** ▲ COOK TIME MINUTES **10** ▲ SERVES **4**

- 3 tablespoons unsalted butter, divided
- 1 pound asparagus, bottom inch trimmed
- 1 pound jumbo shrimp, peeled and deveined
- 1 teaspoon garlic herb seasoning
- ¼ teaspoon kosher salt
- ⅛ teaspoon ground black pepper
- 2 tablespoons lemon juice

1. Preheat griddle to medium. Add 1½ tablespoons butter and, once melted, add asparagus. Cook 4 minutes, turning with tongs a few times.
2. Add remaining 1½ tablespoons butter to empty side of griddle and, once melted, add shrimp. Sprinkle garlic herb seasoning, salt, and pepper on both shrimp and asparagus. Cook 4 more minutes, flipping shrimp halfway through the cooking time and continuing to turn asparagus.
3. Add lemon juice over shrimp and asparagus and serve immediately.

PER SERVING: Calories: 160 | Fat: 8g | Sodium: 764mg | Carbohydrates: 5g | Fiber: 1g | Sugar: 1g | Protein: 17g

VEGETABLE OPTIONS

You can substitute other vegetables for the asparagus in this meal. Vegetables with the same cook time include a pound of halved Brussels sprouts, sliced zucchini or summer squash, and broccoli florets. If you'd like to use sliced bell peppers, sliced mushrooms, or green beans, simply cook them for 6 minutes before adding the shrimp because these vegetables have a slightly longer cook time.

EGGPLANT PARMESAN TORTELLINI

This meatless Italian feast is perfect served with garlic toast. Simply place a few slices of frozen, thawed garlic toast on an empty space on the Blackstone and cook each side for a few minutes until golden brown.

PREP TIME MINUTES **5** ▲ COOK TIME MINUTES **12** ▲ SERVES **4**

- 1 (20-ounce) bag frozen cheese tortellini, thawed
- 1 tablespoon olive oil
- 1 medium eggplant, diced
- 1 tablespoon Italian seasoning blend
- 1 teaspoon garlic powder
- ½ teaspoon kosher salt
- ¼ teaspoon ground black pepper
- 2 cups marinara sauce
- 1½ cups shredded mozzarella cheese
- ½ cup shredded Parmesan cheese

1. Preheat griddle to medium. Add tortellini, squirt with 2 tablespoons water, and cover with melting dome or lid for 4 minutes. Flip halfway through the cooking time, adding 2 more tablespoons water before covering again.
2. Add oil, eggplant, Italian seasoning, garlic powder, salt, and pepper. Cook 5 minutes, mixing with spatulas.
3. Add marinara sauce and combine with spatulas for 2 minutes.
4. Sprinkle mozzarella and Parmesan over top. Lower griddle lid or cover with melting dome for 1 minute until cheese is melted. Serve warm.

PER SERVING: Calories: 581 | Fat: 22g | Sodium: 1,489mg | Carbohydrates: 68g | Fiber: 13g | Sugar: 11g | Protein: 29g

Mincing fresh garlic at the campground is no fun, and garlic powder is so easy to pack. But if you prefer fresh garlic, here are a few suggestions: You can use squeezable garlic paste or minced garlic in a jar, or you can mince fresh garlic at home and store it in 2-ounce cups with lids in your cooler, preferably in a plastic bag.

BBQ BEANIE WEENIES

This childhood classic brings comfort and nostalgia to the campground. Tell your kids stories and memories of your childhood while enjoying this meal together.

PREP TIME MINUTES **10** ▲ COOK TIME MINUTES **20** ▲ SERVES **6**

1 tablespoon vegetable oil

1 medium yellow onion, peeled and diced

2 teaspoons barbecue seasoning blend

6 beef hot dogs, cut into 1-inch slices

1 (28-ounce) can baked beans

½ cup barbecue sauce

1. Preheat griddle to medium. Add oil, onion, and seasoning. Cook 5 minutes, mixing with spatulas. Add hot dogs and cook 3 more minutes.
2. Transfer onions and hot dogs to a 9" × 13" foil pan. Scrape griddle clean and then place pan on griddle. Add baked beans and barbecue sauce.
3. Cook 12 minutes, mixing with a spoon a few times.
4. Serve in bowls once hot and bubbly.

PER SERVING: Calories: 341 | Fat: 16g | Sodium: 1,273mg | Carbohydrates: 41g | Fiber: 6g | Sugar: 20g | Protein: 12g

SAUSAGE AND SHRIMP KEBABS WITH RICE

This is a nice, light meal with a beautiful presentation. Don't feel like messing with kebabs? Simply put all the ingredients on the Blackstone for a stir-fry that will be ready in the same amount of time.

PREP TIME MINUTES **5** ▲ COOK TIME MINUTES **8** ▲ SERVES **4**

- **1 pound jumbo shrimp, peeled and deveined**
- **1 pound smoked sausage, cut into 1-inch slices**
- **1 teaspoon Cajun seasoning blend**
- **2 tablespoons olive oil, divided**
- **1 (17.3-ounce) pouch Ben's Cilantro Lime Ready Rice**
- **½ cup remoulade sauce**

1. Place shrimp and sausage onto kebab skewers, alternating them. Season both sides with Cajun seasoning.
2. Preheat griddle to medium. Add 1 tablespoon oil and rice with ¼ cup water. Lower griddle lid or cover with melting dome for 2 minutes.
3. To the empty side of griddle, add remaining 1 tablespoon oil and kebabs. Cook 6 minutes, flipping kebabs halfway through the cooking time and mixing rice with spatulas a few times.
4. Remove rice to plates and place kebabs over rice. Drizzle with remoulade sauce before serving.

PER SERVING: Calories: 818 | Fat: 54g | Sodium: 2,111mg | Carbohydrates: 41g | Fiber: 3g | Sugar: 4g | Protein: 33g

TACO CHICKEN AND STREET CORN

Everyone does tacos while camping, right?! But not everyone takes taco night to the next level like this tasty dish does. Pickled red onions and lime wedges make yummy additions.

PREP TIME MINUTES **10** ▲ COOK TIME MINUTES **8** ▲ SERVES **4**

4 (5-ounce) thin-cut, boneless, skinless chicken breasts

1½ tablespoons taco seasoning blend, divided

2 tablespoons vegetable oil, divided

2 (14-ounce) cans corn, drained

½ cup sour cream

½ cup chopped cilantro

¼ cup crumbled cotija cheese

1. Season chicken on both sides with half of the taco seasoning.
2. Preheat griddle to medium. Add 1 tablespoon oil and chicken. Cook 4 minutes and flip.
3. To an empty space on griddle, add remaining 1 tablespoon oil, corn, and remaining taco seasoning. Cook 4 more minutes, mixing corn a few times with spatulas.
4. Add sour cream and cilantro to corn and combine with spatulas.
5. Remove chicken and top with street corn mixture. Serve with cotija sprinkled over top.

PER SERVING: Calories: 405 | Fat: 18g | Sodium: 616mg | Carbohydrates: 20g | Fiber: 0g | Sugar: 1g | Protein: 36g

ADJUSTING YOUR SEASONING

Most store-bought seasoning blends already contain salt. If your seasoning blend does not, then you may need to adjust by adding some salt. As with any of these recipes, feel free to add more or less seasoning blend, salt, and/or pepper according to your preferences. If you like things spicy, add crushed red pepper flakes, or leave them out of a recipe that calls for them for a milder version.

SPINACH AND TOMATO RAVIOLI

This dish is a creamy, delicious vegetarian Blackstone meal. Who knew you could enjoy a complete pasta dinner while camping?!

PREP TIME MINUTES **5** ▲ COOK TIME MINUTES **10** ▲ SERVES **4**

1 (20-ounce) bag frozen cheese ravioli, thawed

1 tablespoon olive oil

1 pint whole grape tomatoes

1 (10-ounce) bag spinach leaves

½ teaspoon kosher salt

¼ teaspoon ground black pepper

1 tablespoon Italian seasoning blend

1 (16-ounce) jar Alfredo sauce

1. Preheat griddle to medium. Add ravioli, squirt with 2 tablespoons water, and lower griddle lid or cover with melting dome. Cook 2 minutes, mixing halfway through the cooking time and adding 2 more tablespoons water before covering again.
2. Add oil and tomatoes to ravioli. Cook 4 minutes, combining with spatulas.
3. Add spinach, salt, and pepper. Mix with spatulas and cook 3 more minutes.
4. Add Italian seasoning and Alfredo sauce, mix, and cook 1 more minute. Serve warm

PER SERVING: Calories: 512 | Fat: 30g | Sodium: 1,309mg | Carbohydrates: 49g | Fiber: 4g | Sugar: 4g | Protein: 17g

BBQ CHICKEN BITES AND CORN

Sometimes the best camping meals are the ones with zero fuss. This dish is always a favorite and is ridiculously simple and stress-free, especially if you prepare the chicken at home and store it in a plastic bag.

PREP TIME MINUTES **10** ▲ COOK TIME MINUTES **11** ▲ SERVES **4**

1½ pounds boneless, skinless chicken breasts, cut into bite-sized pieces

2 tablespoons Worcestershire sauce

2 tablespoons barbecue seasoning blend, divided

2 tablespoons olive oil, divided

4 ears corn, shucked

½ cup barbecue sauce

1. Put chicken in a gallon-sized plastic bag with Worcestershire sauce and 1½ tablespoons barbecue seasoning. Massage bag until ingredients are combined.
2. Preheat griddle to medium. Add 1 tablespoon oil to one side of griddle and add corn. Use tongs to rotate corn to coat with oil, season all sides with remaining ½ tablespoon barbecue seasoning, and cook 2 minutes.
3. Add remaining 1 tablespoon oil to the other side of griddle and add chicken. Cook 8–9 minutes, rotating corn a few times and mixing chicken with spatulas. Remove once corn is tender and chicken is cooked through.
4. Serve with barbecue sauce for dipping.

PER SERVING: Calories: 223 | Fat: 3g | Sodium: 1,012mg | Carbohydrates: 18g | Fiber: 1g | Sugar: 13g | Protein: 31g

FLAVOR VARIATIONS

You can create new variations of this meal by using different seasoning blends in place of the barbecue seasoning and mixing it up with a variety of sauces. Blackstone has Honey Jalapeño, Parmesan Ranch, and Lemon Peppercorn seasonings that all pair great with ranch dressing. Some other Blackstone seasonings include the Island Stir Fry or Pineapple Sriracha seasoning with Caribbean Jerk sauce for dipping. Or try a taco seasoning served with sour cream mixed with salsa, or Cajun seasoning with remoulade sauce

VEGETABLE HUMMUS LAVASH FLATBREADS

Lavash flatbreads are so light, and the Blackstone griddle creates such a thin, crisp crust. Topping ideas are endless, so get as creative as you like. Feta or goat cheese crumbles are great additions as well.

PREP TIME MINUTES **10** ▲ COOK TIME MINUTES **12** ▲ SERVES **4**

- 2 tablespoons olive oil, divided
- 8 ounces baby portobello mushrooms, sliced
- 1 medium red bell pepper, seeded and sliced
- ¼ teaspoon kosher salt
- ⅛ teaspoon ground black pepper
- 3 cups chopped spinach
- 1 teaspoon garlic powder
- 1 teaspoon dried oregano
- 3 tablespoons balsamic vinegar
- 4 lavash flatbreads
- 1 cup hummus, at room temperature

1. Preheat griddle to medium. Add 1 tablespoon oil, mushrooms, bell pepper, salt, and pepper. Cook 5 minutes, mixing with spatulas.
2. Add spinach, garlic powder, oregano, and balsamic vinegar. Mix and cook another 3 minutes.
3. Remove vegetables from griddle and scrape griddle clean. Add remaining 1 tablespoon oil and flatbreads (depending on griddle size, you may need to cook these 2 at a time). Cook 2 minutes per side or until crisped to your liking.
4. Remove flatbreads and let cool 2 minutes. Assemble flatbreads by spreading hummus on top and adding vegetables evenly. Slice and serve.

PER SERVING: Calories: 501 | Fat: 13g | Sodium: 858mg | Carbohydrates: 77g | Fiber: 5g | Sugar: 6g | Protein: 17g

CAPRESE CHICKEN AND GARLIC TOAST

This complete and luxurious meal gives off fancy Italian restaurant vibes even though you're enjoying an evening under the stars! Serve with a glass of wine to complete the mood.

PREP TIME MINUTES **5** ▲ COOK TIME MINUTES **8** ▲ SERVES **4**

- 2 tablespoons olive oil
- 4 (5-ounce) thin-cut, boneless, skinless chicken breasts
- 1 pint whole grape tomatoes
- 1 teaspoon garlic herb seasoning
- ½ teaspoon kosher salt
- ¼ teaspoon ground black pepper
- 4 slices frozen garlic toast, thawed
- 1 cup shredded mozzarella cheese
- 4 tablespoons pesto

1. Preheat griddle to medium. Add oil and chicken to one side of griddle. On the other side, add tomatoes. Sprinkle garlic herb seasoning, salt, and pepper on both chicken and tomatoes.
2. Cook chicken and tomatoes 7 minutes, flipping chicken halfway through the cooking time and mixing tomatoes a few times with spatulas.
3. After flipping chicken, add garlic toast to griddle. Flip a few times and remove once toasted and golden brown.
4. Sprinkle cheese on chicken and cover with melting dome for 1 minute until cheese melts.
5. Serve cheesy chicken topped with dollops of pesto and tomatoes. Serve garlic toast on the side.

PER SERVING: Calories: 505 | Fat: 27g | Sodium: 863mg | Carbohydrates: 24g | Fiber: 2g | Sugar: 3g | Protein: 41g

UNSTUFFED BELL PEPPERS

Sure, stuffed peppers are great, but stuffing peppers while camping? Not so much fun. With this recipe, you can enjoy all the flavors of stuffed peppers without the fuss. Any color bell pepper works, so just use your favorite.

PREP TIME MINUTES **10** ▲ COOK TIME MINUTES **12** ▲ SERVES **4**

- **1 tablespoon olive oil**
- **2 medium green bell peppers, seeded and sliced**
- **½ teaspoon kosher salt**
- **¼ teaspoon ground black pepper**
- **1 pound ground Italian sausage**
- **1 teaspoon Italian seasoning blend**
- **½ teaspoon garlic powder**
- **1 (8.8-ounce) pouch Ben's Spanish Style Ready Rice**
- **1 cup marinara sauce**
- **1 cup shredded mozzarella cheese**

1. Preheat griddle to medium. Add oil, bell peppers, salt, and pepper. Cook 3 minutes, mixing with spatulas.
2. Add sausage, Italian seasoning, garlic powder, rice, and ¼ cup water. Cook 7 more minutes, breaking sausage apart with spatulas and mixing everything together.
3. Add marinara sauce and cheese and combine with spatulas 2 more minutes. Serve warm.

PER SERVING: Calories: 571 | Fat: 34g | Sodium: 1,822mg | Carbohydrates: 34g | Fiber: 2g | Sugar: 6g | Protein: 27g

COWBOY SAUSAGE HASH

This is a hearty meal to end a day of fun in the great outdoors. Add your favorite all-purpose seasoning blend to give this hash even more personality.

PREP TIME MINUTES **10** ▲ COOK TIME MINUTES **15** ▲ SERVES **4**

2 tablespoons olive oil, divided

1 (20-ounce) bag diced Simply Potatoes

1 medium yellow onion, peeled and sliced

1 medium red bell pepper, seeded and sliced

1 teaspoon garlic powder

½ teaspoon kosher salt

¼ teaspoon ground black pepper

1 pound smoked sausage, cut into 1-inch slices

1. Preheat griddle to medium. Add 1 tablespoon oil, potatoes, and ¼ cup water. Lower griddle lid or cover with melting dome. Cook potatoes 5 minutes, adding ¼ cup more water and mixing halfway through the cooking time. Raise lid or set dome aside.
2. Add remaining 1 tablespoon oil, onion, bell pepper, garlic powder, salt, and pepper. Cook 5 more minutes, combining with spatulas.
3. Add sausage and cook 5 more minutes, mixing a few times. Serve warm.

PER SERVING: Calories: 534 | Fat: 34g | Sodium: 1,290mg | Carbohydrates: 33g | Fiber: 4g | Sugar: 2g | Protein: 17g

GREEK SHRIMP WITH NAAN

This dish will remind you of a deconstructed gyro. You could use 1-inch cubes of lamb or chicken in place of the shrimp; just add 3–4 minutes to the shrimp cook time. Garnish with fresh parsley and lemon wedges if desired.

PREP TIME MINUTES **5** ▲ COOK TIME MINUTES **6** ▲ SERVES **4**

1½ pounds jumbo shrimp, peeled and deveined

2 tablespoons olive oil

½ teaspoon kosher salt

½ teaspoon smoked paprika

½ teaspoon dried oregano

½ teaspoon garlic powder

1 (7.05-ounce) 4-pack mini naan flatbreads

8 ounces tzatziki sauce

1. Put shrimp in a medium bowl with oil, salt, paprika, oregano, and garlic powder. Toss until combined.
2. Preheat griddle to medium. Add shrimp and cook 4–5 minutes, mixing with spatulas a few times, until shrimp are cooked through.
3. Place flatbreads on an empty space on griddle for 30 seconds per side to warm them.
4. Serve shrimp with naan on the side and tzatziki sauce on the side for dipping, or assemble bites combining torn naan pieces and shrimp.

PER SERVING: Calories: 403 | Fat: 14g | Sodium: 1,784mg | Carbohydrates: 33g | Fiber: 1g | Sugar: 6g | Protein: 32g

MEATBALL RICOTTA PIZZA

Ricotta is an often-overlooked but fabulous pizza topping. Add meatballs and a soft, pillowy naan bread crust, and this pizza is pure bliss.

PREP TIME MINUTES **5** ▲ COOK TIME MINUTES **11** ▲ SERVES **4**

10 frozen Italian meatballs, thawed and cut in half

2 (4-ounce) naan flatbreads

¾ cup pizza sauce

1 cup shredded mozzarella cheese

1 cup ricotta cheese

1 teaspoon Italian seasoning blend

½ teaspoon garlic powder

1. Preheat griddle to medium-low. Add meatballs and lower griddle lid or cover with melting dome for 5 minutes, mixing a few times. Scoot meatballs to edge of griddle.
2. Place flatbreads on griddle for 1 minute and then flip them.
3. Spread pizza sauce on flatbreads and top with mozzarella, dollops of ricotta, meatballs, Italian seasoning, and garlic powder. Lower griddle lid or cover with melting dome 3–5 minutes or until cheese is melted.
4. Let cool slightly, slice, and serve.

PER SERVING: Calories: 503 | Fat: 25g | Sodium: 1,118mg | Carbohydrates: 40g | Fiber: 3g | Sugar: 7g | Protein: 25g

TORTELLINI AND HAM ALFREDO

This one is always popular with the kids. Mix in a cup of shredded mozzarella when adding the Alfredo sauce or serve with Parmesan to add some cheesy goodness.

PREP TIME MINUTES **5** ▲ COOK TIME MINUTES **11** ▲ SERVES **4**

- **1 (20-ounce) bag frozen cheese tortellini, thawed**
- **2 tablespoons unsalted butter**
- **1 pound ham steak, cubed**
- **1 cup frozen peas**
- **1 (16-ounce) jar Alfredo sauce**
- **1 tablespoon Italian seasoning blend**

1. Preheat griddle to medium. Add tortellini, squirt with 2 tablespoons water, and cover with melting dome or lid for 4 minutes. Flip halfway through the cooking time, adding 2 more tablespoons water before covering again.
2. Add butter to tortellini and, once melted, add ham. Cook 4 minutes, mixing with spatulas.
3. Add peas, Alfredo sauce, and Italian seasoning. Cook 2 more minutes, combining all ingredients. Serve warm.

PER SERVING: Calories: 754 | Fat: 37g | Sodium: 1,284mg | Carbohydrates: 59g | Fiber: 10g | Sugar: 3g | Protein: 49g

POT ROAST STIR-FRY

Pot roast is usually cooked low and slow, but this quick Blackstone version will give you all the same flavors without all the waiting.

PREP TIME MINUTES **10** ▲ COOK TIME MINUTES **15** ▲ SERVES **4**

2 tablespoons olive oil, divided

1 (20-ounce) bag diced Simply Potatoes

1 (12-ounce) bag baby carrots

1 medium yellow onion, peeled and sliced

1 pound sirloin steak, cut into bite-sized pieces

1 (1-ounce) packet pot roast seasoning

1 (12-ounce) jar beef gravy

1. Preheat griddle to medium. Add 1 tablespoon oil, potatoes, carrots, and ¼ cup water, and lower griddle lid or cover with melting dome. Cook 6 minutes, adding ¼ cup more water and mixing halfway through the cooking time. Raise lid or set dome aside.
2. Add onion and remaining 1 tablespoon oil and cook 4 minutes, mixing everything together with spatulas.
3. Add steak and pot roast seasoning and cook 4 more minutes, mixing a few times. Pour gravy over top and combine with spatulas 1 more minute. Serve warm.

PER SERVING: Calories: 491 | Fat: 19g | Sodium: 1,309mg | Carbohydrates: 45g | Fiber: 5g | Sugar: 5g | Protein: 29g

CAJUN CATFISH AND CHIPS

Fish and chips are a fantastic combo. If the catfish is your fresh catch of the day, it's even better! You can swap out trout, tilapia, or flounder, as they all have the same cook time as catfish.

PREP TIME MINUTES **5** ▲ COOK TIME MINUTES **10** ▲ SERVES **4**

- **4 (6-ounce) catfish fillets**
- **2 teaspoons Cajun seasoning blend, divided**
- **2 tablespoons vegetable oil**
- **1 (24-ounce) bag frozen French fries, thawed**
- **½ cup tartar sauce**

1. Pat fish dry and season both sides with 1 teaspoon Cajun seasoning.
2. Preheat griddle to medium-low. Add oil, put fries on one side of griddle, and sprinkle with remaining 1 teaspoon Cajun seasoning. Add fish on the other side. Cook fries and fish 8–10 minutes total, flipping everything a few times with spatulas.
3. Remove once fish is cooked through and fries are crisped to your liking. Serve with tartar sauce for dipping.

PER SERVING: Calories: 517 | Fat: 23g | Sodium: 863mg | Carbohydrates: 42g | Fiber: 3g | Sugar: 0g | Protein: 30g

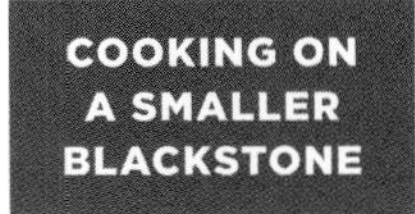

If you have a smaller Blackstone, you may need to adjust how to cook bigger meals. If all the ingredients won't fit at once, cook one part of a meal and set it aside while you cook the other half of the meal. Warm up anything that has been set aside for a minute or two on the griddle before serving.

HIBACHI STEAK KEBABS

An entire hibachi-style meal at the campground can be a little involved, but these kebabs are simple and can even be prepared at home and stored in a sealed container until ready to cook.

PREP TIME MINUTES **70*** ▲ COOK TIME MINUTES **10** ▲ SERVES **4**

- 1 pound sirloin steak, cut into 1-inch cubes
- 2 tablespoons soy sauce
- 1 medium zucchini, cut into 1-inch slices
- 1 medium yellow onion, peeled and cut into 1-inch pieces
- 4 ounces white mushrooms
- ½ teaspoon garlic powder
- ½ teaspoon kosher salt
- ¼ teaspoon ground black pepper
- 2 tablespoons vegetable oil
- ¾ cup yum yum sauce

* INCLUDES MARINATING TIME

1. Put steak in a medium bowl with soy sauce. Toss until combined and marinate 1 hour.
2. Assemble kebabs on four wooden or metal skewers, alternating steak with zucchini, onion, and mushrooms. Season all sides with garlic powder, salt, and pepper.
3. Preheat griddle to medium. Add oil and place kebabs onto griddle. Cook 8–10 minutes total, turning kebabs with tongs a few times until steak and vegetables are cooked to your liking.
4. Serve with yum yum sauce on the side for dipping.

PER SERVING: Calories: 537 | Fat: 43g | Sodium: 1,006mg | Carbohydrates: 13g | Fiber: 1g | Sugar: 10g | Protein: 27g

ITALIAN SAUSAGE AND KALE SOUP

Soup on the Blackstone may seem crazy, but it works well if you pack a 5-quart soup pot. There is nothing like a warm bowl of comfort, especially when you're camping in the fall.

PREP TIME MINUTES **10** ▲ COOK TIME MINUTES **16** ▲ SERVES **6**

1 tablespoon olive oil

1 (12-ounce) bag frozen diced onion and peppers, thawed

1 pound ground Italian sausage

4 cups chopped kale

1½ tablespoons garlic and herb seasoning blend, divided

4 cups chicken broth

1 (15-ounce) can diced Italian tomatoes

1 (15-ounce) can cannellini beans, drained and rinsed

1 cup heavy cream

1. Preheat griddle to medium. Add oil, onion and peppers, sausage, kale, and ½ tablespoon garlic and herb seasoning. Cook 6 minutes, mixing with spatulas and breaking sausage apart. Remove ingredients from griddle and place in a 5-quart soup pot.
2. Scrape griddle clean and raise heat to high. Place soup pot on griddle and add remaining 1 tablespoon garlic and herb seasoning, chicken broth, tomatoes, beans, and cream.
3. Bring to a boil and cook 10 minutes, stirring several times. You can lower griddle heat to medium-high if soup is bubbling too much.
4. Let cool slightly before serving in bowls.

PER SERVING: Calories: 516 | Fat: 36g | Sodium: 2,075mg | Carbohydrates: 21g | Fiber: 5g | Sugar: 6g | Protein: 21g

PEANUT CHICKEN RICE BOWLS

This one packs a punch of flavor with just a few ingredients, making it a fabulous camping meal. Optional topping ideas are sriracha, chopped peanuts, and lime wedges to squeeze over the top.

PREP TIME MINUTES **10** ▲ COOK TIME MINUTES **10** ▲ SERVES **4**

2 tablespoons vegetable oil, divided

1 (17.3-ounce) pouch Ben's Cilantro Lime Ready Rice

1½ pounds boneless, skinless chicken thighs, cut into bite-sized pieces

½ teaspoon kosher salt

1 cup peanut sauce

2 tablespoons soy sauce

1. Preheat griddle to medium. Add 1 tablespoon oil, rice, and ¼ cup water. Lower griddle lid or cover with melting dome for 2 minutes.
2. Scoot rice to one side of griddle, then add remaining 1 tablespoon oil, chicken, and salt. Cook chicken 6 minutes, mixing with spatulas, and mix rice a few times.
3. Add peanut sauce and soy sauce to chicken, mix, and cook 2 more minutes.
4. Remove rice and place in bowls. Top rice with chicken and peanut sauce. Serve warm.

PER SERVING: Calories: 657 | Fat: 31g | Sodium: 2,015mg | Carbohydrates: 51g | Fiber: 4g | Sugar: 14g | Protein: 38g

You can create this same meal but with a different flavor profile simply by switching out the peanut sauce. Some sauces that would work well are Japanese barbecue, pad Thai sauce, and sweet chili sauce. Or check out any of the stir-fry sauces in the Asian section of your grocery store. You can even get creative and mix two sauces together for your own unique twist.

DESSERTS

When most people think of cooking on the Blackstone, they think of grilling meats and sautéing vegetables, but they tend to not think of desserts. But the truth is, you can cook so many sweet and delicious desserts on your griddle! The griddle is an ideal place to roast fruits, cook all kinds of s'mores, and even make cakes and cookies! In this chapter, you will find all the tasty treats to satisfy your sweet tooth, including Ooey Gooey S'mores Sandwiches, Chocolate Dirt Cake, Easy Beignets, Bourbon Peaches and Cream, Frosted Sugar Cookies, Donut Whoopie Pies, and Fruit and Cake Kebabs. All great camping days should end on a sweet note, so why not make some of these fun and tasty desserts on your Blackstone!

OOEY GOOEY S'MORES SANDWICHES

This dish takes basic s'mores to the next level: They are crispy on the outside and melty on the inside. This recipe is from Erin at @campinerin; follow her on all socials for camping tips, tricks, and shenanigans!

PREP TIME MINUTES **10** ▲ COOK TIME MINUTES **6** ▲ SERVES **4**

- 2 tablespoons unsalted butter, at room temperature
- 4 slices brioche
- ¼ cup semisweet chocolate chips
- ½ cup mini marshmallows
- 2 tablespoons crushed graham crackers
- ½ teaspoon ground cinnamon

1. Spread butter on one side of each slice of bread.
2. Preheat griddle to medium-low. Place two slices of bread, buttered side down, on griddle.
3. Evenly sprinkle both slices with chocolate chips, marshmallows, graham crackers, and cinnamon. Top each with remaining bread slices, buttered side up. Use a spatula or burger press to flatten sandwiches slightly.
4. Lower griddle lid or cover with melting dome. Cook 2–3 minutes per side until bread is golden brown and the filling is ooey, gooey, and melted.
5. Let cool slightly, slice, and serve.

PER SERVING: Calories: 247 | Fat: 10g | Sodium: 209mg | Carbohydrates: 36g | Fiber: 1g | Sugar: 13g | Protein: 4g

CANDY CONES

A messy sweet treat is always a fun way to end your day of camping. And while this recipe is delicious as is, you can also add chocolate chips, a chopped candy bar, or toffee chips for different versions.

PREP TIME MINUTES **10** ▲ COOK TIME MINUTES **5** ▲ SERVES **8**

8 sugar cones

1 cup mini marshmallows

1 cup M&M's

1. Fill each cone evenly with marshmallows and M&M'S, alternating between marshmallows and candy. Smash them down gently to fit as much as possible. Wrap each cone individually in foil.
2. Preheat griddle to medium-low. Place the foil packets on griddle for 5 minutes, turning with tongs a few times. Unwrap before serving.

PER SERVING: Calories: 187 | Fat: 5g | Sodium: 50mg | Carbohydrates: 32g | Fiber: 1g | Sugar: 23g | Protein: 2g

CHOCOLATE DIRT CAKE

Here is a fun and chocolatey dessert that is sure to make the kids smile. Use a disposable foil pan for easy campsite cleanup.

PREP TIME MINUTES **10** ▲ COOK TIME MINUTES **6** ▲ SERVES **8**

1 (13.25-ounce) box chocolate cake mix

½ cup vegetable oil

3 large eggs

3 tablespoons unsalted butter

1 (13-ounce) 4-pack chocolate pudding cups

16 gummy worms

1. To a medium bowl, add cake mix, 1 cup water, oil, and eggs. Stir 2 minutes with a spoon.
2. Preheat griddle to medium-low. Add butter and, once melted, pour cake mix onto griddle. Use spatulas to mix and scramble the batter for 5 minutes until it's crumbly.
3. Spread pudding in the bottom of a 9" × 13" casserole dish. Add cake crumbles evenly over top and place gummy worms in the "dirt."
4. Serve in bowls with spoons.

PER SERVING: Calories: 492 | Fat: 24g | Sodium: 457mg | Carbohydrates: 61g | Fiber: 1g | Sugar: 34g | Protein: 7g

SALTED CARAMEL PRETZEL BITES

You can make these bites when you arrive at your camping destination and store them in a plastic bag to enjoy a sweet and salty treat anytime. This recipe uses pretzel snaps, which are the pretzels that look like waffles.

PREP TIME MINUTES **5** ▲ COOK TIME MINUTES **5** ▲ SERVES **12**

48 pretzel snaps

24 Rolo Creamy Caramels

1. Preheat griddle to low. Place 24 pretzel snaps on griddle, spaced ½ inch apart. Put a Rolo on the center of each pretzel and lower griddle lid or cover with melting dome 5 minutes.
2. Put another pretzel on top of each Rolo and press slightly to smash into a sandwich.
3. Turn griddle off and let bites cool completely before removing and serving.

PER SERVING: Calories: 76 | Fat: 2g | Sodium: 78mg | Carbohydrates: 12g | Fiber: 0g | Sugar: 8g | Protein: 1g

EASY BEIGNETS

A New Orleans classic, a traditional beignet is a deep-fried, pillowy-soft dough. Thanks to the Blackstone, you can enjoy this simple dessert while camping. Enjoy these as is or dip them in chocolate sauce.

PREP TIME MINUTES **10** ▲ COOK TIME MINUTES **9** ▲ SERVES **4**

1 (8-ounce, 8-count) tube crescent rolls

2 tablespoons unsalted butter

2 tablespoons confectioners' sugar

1. Unroll crescent dough triangles and cut each into thirds; any shape is fine as long as they are similar in size.
2. Preheat griddle to medium-low. Add butter and, once melted, place pieces of dough in a single layer, not touching.
3. Lower griddle lid or cover with melting dome 6–8 minutes. Flip the dough a few times with a spatula.
4. Remove once dough is cooked through and golden brown. Sprinkle confectioners' sugar over top right away, and serve warm.

PER SERVING: Calories: 268 | Fat: 15g | Sodium: 425mg | Carbohydrates: 28g | Fiber: 0g | Sugar: 10g | Protein: 4g

CINNAMON WHISKEY APPLE CAKES

This grown-up dessert never disappoints. It is very good topped off with whipped cream or vanilla ice cream. For a non-boozy version, add an extra tablespoon of brown sugar and a pinch of ground cinnamon in place of the whiskey.

PREP TIME MINUTES **10** ▲ COOK TIME MINUTES **9** ▲ SERVES **6**

2 large Honeycrisp apples, unpeeled, cored, and diced

4 tablespoons unsalted butter

2 tablespoons light brown sugar

¼ cup cinnamon whiskey

1 (5-ounce, 6-count) package cake shells

1. Preheat griddle to medium. Put apples on griddle and cook 4 minutes, mixing a few times with spatulas.
2. Add butter, brown sugar, and cinnamon whiskey. Cook 4 more minutes, mixing with spatulas.
3. Place cake shells on an empty space on griddle for 1 minute to warm them.
4. Remove shells and serve topped with cinnamon whiskey apples.

PER SERVING: Calories: 193 | Fat: 7g | Sodium: 96mg | Carbohydrates: 27g | Fiber: 2g | Sugar: 19g | Protein: 1g

STRAWBERRY NUTELLA DESSERT PIZZA

This sweet version of pizza is a nice way to end the evening around the campfire. Keep in mind, this dish does require a few extra napkins.

PREP TIME MINUTES **10** ▲ COOK TIME MINUTES **5** ▲ SERVES **4**

5 ounces Nutella

2 (4-ounce) naan flatbreads

1 cup sliced strawberries

⅓ cup white chocolate chips

1. Spread Nutella evenly on each flatbread.
2. Preheat griddle to medium-low. Put flatbreads on griddle, Nutella side up.
3. Sprinkle strawberries and white chocolate chips evenly over top of flatbreads. Lower griddle lid or cover with melting dome 4–5 minutes until chocolate starts to melt.
4. Remove and let cool for 2 minutes before slicing and serving.

PER SERVING: Calories: 451 | Fat: 19g | Sodium: 472mg | Carbohydrates: 61g | Fiber: 3g | Sugar: 33g | Protein: 9g

TWINKIE STRAWBERRY SHORTCAKE

This recipe takes the classic Twinkie to a whole new level. A little extra whipped cream over the top is never a bad thing if the Twinkie filling just isn't enough for you.

PREP TIME MINUTES **10** ▲ COOK TIME MINUTES **5** ▲ SERVES **6**

1 pint strawberries, stems removed and sliced

1 tablespoon granulated sugar

1 tablespoon lemon juice

6 Twinkies

1. Preheat griddle to medium-low. Add strawberries and cook 1 minute, mixing with spatulas.
2. Add sugar and lemon juice. Cook 4 more minutes, mixing. During the last minute of cooking time, put Twinkies on an empty space on griddle to warm them.
3. Remove Twinkies, top with strawberries, and serve.

PER SERVING: Calories: 167 | Fat: 5g | Sodium: 180mg | Carbohydrates: 31g | Fiber: 1g | Sugar: 20g | Protein: 1g

BOURBON PEACHES AND CREAM

The bourbon in this recipe screams camping party vibes, but you can leave the bourbon out if you'd prefer. Try to use peaches that are ripe but still firm.

PREP TIME MINUTES **10** ▲ COOK TIME MINUTES **9** ▲ SERVES **4**

- 3 tablespoons unsalted butter
- 4 medium peaches, pitted and sliced
- 2 tablespoons bourbon
- 3 tablespoons light brown sugar
- ¼ teaspoon ground cinnamon
- 4 ounces whipped cream

1. Preheat griddle to medium-low. Add butter and, once melted, add peaches. Cook 4 minutes, mixing a few times with spatulas.
2. Add bourbon, brown sugar, and cinnamon to peaches. Cook 3–4 more minutes until peaches are tender and sauce is caramelized.
3. Remove from griddle, let cool slightly, and top with whipped cream to serve.

PER SERVING: Calories: 255 | Fat: 14g | Sodium: 6mg | Carbohydrates: 28g | Fiber: 2g | Sugar: 25g | Protein: 2g

You can serve these peaches, or any griddled fruit topping, over warm slices of buttery pound cake. With the Blackstone over medium-low heat, add 1 tablespoon unsalted butter. Once melted, place several 1-inch-thick slices of pound cake on the griddle for 1–2 minutes per side until golden brown and slightly toasted. Serve the fruit over the pound cake and top with whipped cream.

PINEAPPLE UPSIDE-DOWN CAKES

This dessert features the cake shells usually used for strawberry shortcake that can easily be found in the bakery section of most larger grocery stores. Sliced pound cake is a great substitution.

PREP TIME MINUTES **5** ▲ COOK TIME MINUTES **5** ▲ SERVES **6**

2 tablespoons unsalted butter

1 (20-ounce) can pineapple tidbits, drained

3 tablespoons light brown sugar

1 (5-ounce, 6-count) package cake shells

6 maraschino cherries

1. Preheat griddle to medium. Add butter and, once melted, add pineapple and brown sugar. Cook 3–4 minutes until pineapple is warm and bubbly.
2. While pineapple cooks, place cakes on an empty space on griddle and cook 1 minute per side.
3. Remove cakes and top each with pineapple mixture and a cherry. Serve.

PER SERVING: Calories: 167 | Fat: 4g | Sodium: 96mg | Carbohydrates: 33g | Fiber: 1g | Sugar: 26g | Protein: 1g

FROSTED SUGAR COOKIES

You will need a baking sheet and a piece of parchment paper for this recipe. This baking method on the Blackstone works with any type of "break-and-bake" cookie dough.

PREP TIME MINUTES **5** ▲ COOK TIME MINUTES **15** ▲ SERVES **12**

- 1 (16-ounce, 24-count) package sugar cookie dough
- 1 (16-ounce) container vanilla frosting
- 2 ounces rainbow sprinkles

1. Preheat griddle to low. Place a baking sheet upside down on Blackstone and lay a piece of parchment paper on it.
2. Break cookie dough apart and place the pieces on the parchment paper, spaced ½ inch apart.
3. Lower griddle lid or cover with large melting dome for 10–15 minutes. Remove once the cookies are cooked through. Let cool.
4. Spread frosting on cookies and then top with sprinkles. Serve.

PER SERVING: Calories: 336 | Fat: 14g | Sodium: 179mg | Carbohydrates: 53g | Fiber: 0g | Sugar: 41g | Protein: 2g

COOKIE DECORATING IDEAS

Decorating these cookies can be a fun camping activity the whole family can participate in. Pack some different colors of frosting and a variety of sprinkles. You could also create a toppings bar with candy such as mini chocolate chips, toffee bits, crushed candy canes, or mini M&M's.

S'MORES BANANA SPLITS

The best bananas to use for this sweet treat are ones that are all yellow with no brown spots and no green color on the peel.

PREP TIME MINUTES **5** ▲ COOK TIME MINUTES **6** ▲ SERVES **4**

4 large bananas, unpeeled

1 tablespoon unsalted butter

¾ cup semisweet chocolate chips

¾ cup mini marshmallows

½ cup crushed graham crackers

1. Cut unpeeled bananas completely in half lengthwise. Cut a ½-inch slice down the center of each banana half to make a pocket for the filling.
2. Preheat griddle to medium-low. Add butter and, once melted, place banana halves, cut side down, on griddle for 2 minutes.
3. Flip bananas and stuff the chocolate chips and marshmallows into the slices of each banana half. Lower griddle lid or cover with melting dome 3 more minutes until chocolate and marshmallows are slightly melted.
4. Remove, sprinkle crushed graham crackers over top, and serve each banana with a spoon.

PER SERVING: Calories: 384 | Fat: 14g | Sodium: 60mg | Carbohydrates: 69g | Fiber: 6g | Sugar: 43g | Protein: 4g

FRUIT AND CAKE KEBABS

This light dessert is extra fun to prepare with friends or the kids. Seeing who can make the prettiest kebab is a nice, friendly camping competition. Fresh mint is an optional garnish.

PREP TIME MINUTES **10** ▲ COOK TIME MINUTES **6** ▲ SERVES **8**

- 1 (10-ounce) pound cake loaf, cut into 1-inch cubes
- 1 pint strawberries, stems removed and cut in half
- 1 (20-ounce) can pineapple chunks, drained
- 2 tablespoons unsalted butter
- 1 cup frozen whipped topping, thawed

1. Assemble kebabs on eight wooden or metal skewers by alternating cake and fruit.
2. Preheat griddle to medium-low. Add butter and, once melted, place kebabs on griddle 5 minutes, turning a few times until cake is toasted and fruit is slightly softened and warm.
3. Serve with whipped topping on the side for dipping.

PER SERVING: Calories: 220 | Fat: 8g | Sodium: 134mg | Carbohydrates: 33g | Fiber: 2g | Sugar: 23g | Protein: 2g

Add your own creative touch by using a variety of fruit such as banana slices, grapes, peaches, mango chunks, or raspberries. Stir in some lemon juice to the whipped topping to add a pop of freshness. A drizzle of chocolate sauce is a fun and messy addition.

OREO RICE KRISPIES TREATS

Here is a scrumptious cookies-and-cream version of the classic Rice Krispies Treat. In place of the Oreos, you could add 1 cup peanut butter or ¼ cup colored sprinkles. You can even make a s'mores version by using 1 cup chocolate chips and Golden Grahams cereal instead.

PREP TIME MINUTES **5** ▲ COOK TIME MINUTES **6** ▲ SERVES **8**

4 tablespoons unsalted butter

1 (10-ounce) bag mini marshmallows

6 cups Rice Krispies cereal

12 Oreo cookies, crushed

1. Preheat griddle to medium-low. Place a 9" × 13" foil pan on griddle and add butter.
2. Once butter is melted, lift pan up using towels or heat-proof gloves and tilt pan around to evenly coat the bottom with butter.
3. Add marshmallows and cook 3–5 minutes, stirring a few times until they melt. Turn griddle off and add cereal and cookies.
4. Stir until mixture is evenly combined, which will take a few minutes. Using towels or heat-proof gloves to hold on to the pan makes this easier. Let cool before slicing and serving.

PER SERVING: Calories: 329 | Fat: 9g | Sodium: 213mg | Carbohydrates: 60g | Fiber: 1g | Sugar: 30g | Protein: 3g

DONUT WHOOPIE PIES

This version of a whoopie pie is simplified for camping ease, but it's even better than the store-bought version because it's served warm and ooey gooey straight from the Blackstone.

PREP TIME MINUTES **10** ▲ COOK TIME MINUTES **7** ▲ SERVES **4**

4 chocolate glazed donuts

1 cup marshmallow fluff

2 tablespoons unsalted butter

1. Cut donuts in half lengthwise through the center to separate tops and bottoms.
2. Spread marshmallow fluff on both the bottom and top half of each donut, then sandwich them back together.
3. Preheat griddle to medium-low. Add butter and, once melted, place whoopie pie sandwiches on griddle. Press them down with spatulas or a burger press. Cook 2–3 minutes per side until they are warm and slightly toasted.
4. Serve warm with plenty of napkins.

PER SERVING: Calories: 410 | Fat: 22g | Sodium: 210mg | Carbohydrates: 53g | Fiber: 0g | Sugar: 34g | Protein: 2g

STANDARD US/METRIC MEASUREMENT CONVERSIONS

VOLUME CONVERSIONS

US Volume Measure	Metric Equivalent
⅛ teaspoon	0.5 milliliter
¼ teaspoon	1 milliliter
½ teaspoon	2 milliliters
1 teaspoon	5 milliliters
½ tablespoon	7 milliliters
1 tablespoon (3 teaspoons)	15 milliliters
2 tablespoons (1 fluid ounce)	30 milliliters
¼ cup (4 tablespoons)	60 milliliters
⅓ cup	90 milliliters
½ cup (4 fluid ounces)	125 milliliters
⅔ cup	160 milliliters
¾ cup (6 fluid ounces)	180 milliliters
1 cup (16 tablespoons)	250 milliliters
1 pint (2 cups)	500 milliliters
1 quart (4 cups)	1 liter (about)

WEIGHT CONVERSIONS

US Weight Measure	Metric Equivalent
½ ounce	15 grams
1 ounce	30 grams
2 ounces	60 grams
3 ounces	85 grams
¼ pound (4 ounces)	115 grams
½ pound (8 ounces)	225 grams
¾ pound (12 ounces)	340 grams
1 pound (16 ounces)	454 grams

OVEN TEMPERATURE CONVERSIONS

Degrees Fahrenheit	Degrees Celsius
200 degrees F	95 degrees C
250 degrees F	120 degrees C
275 degrees F	135 degrees C
300 degrees F	150 degrees C
325 degrees F	160 degrees C
350 degrees F	180 degrees C
375 degrees F	190 degrees C
400 degrees F	205 degrees C
425 degrees F	220 degrees C
450 degrees F	230 degrees C

BAKING PAN SIZES

American	Metric
8 × 1½ inch round baking pan	20 × 4 cm cake tin
9 × 1½ inch round baking pan	23 × 3.5 cm cake tin
11 × 7 × 1½ inch baking pan	28 × 18 × 4 cm baking tin
13 × 9 × 2 inch baking pan	30 × 20 × 5 cm baking tin
2 quart rectangular baking dish	30 × 20 × 3 cm baking tin
15 × 10 × 2 inch baking pan	30 × 25 × 2 cm baking tin (Swiss roll tin)
9 inch pie plate	22 × 4 or 23 × 4 cm pie plate
7 or 8 inch springform pan	18 or 20 cm springform or loose bottom cake tin
9 × 5 × 3 inch loaf pan	23 × 13 × 7 cm or 2 lb narrow loaf or pate tin
1½ quart casserole	1.5 liter casserole
2 quart casserole	2 liter casserole

INDEX

C

D

E

F

G

H

I

J

K

L

M

N

O

P

R

S

T

U

V

W

Z

Fire up your griddle and get *sizzling*!

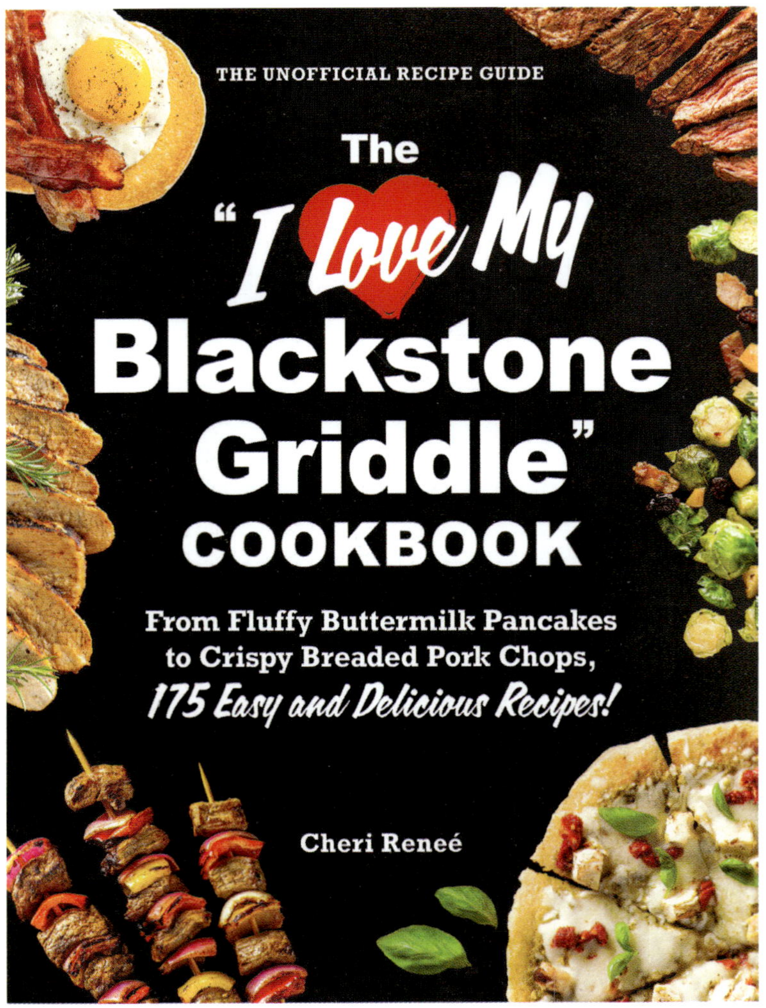

Pick up or download your copy today!